AMERICAN CLASSICIST

THE ARCHITECTURE OF
PHILIP TRAMMELL SHUTZE

AMERICAN CLASSICIST

THE ARCHITECTURE OF
PHILIP TRAMMELL SHUTZE

Elizabeth Meredith Dowling

PREFACE BY HENRY HOPE REED
INTRODUCTION BY VINCENT SCULLY
PHOTOGRAPHY BY TIMOTHY HURSLEY

RIZZOLI
NEW YORK

To Geddes

First published in the United States of America in 1989 by
RIZZOLI INTERNATIONAL PUBLICATIONS, INC.
597 Fifth Avenue, New York, NY 10017

Library of Congress Cataloging-in-Publication Data

Dowling, Elizabeth Meredith.
    American classicist.
    Includes index.
    1. Shutze, Philip Trammell.   2. Architects—
United States—Biography.   3. Classicism in architecture—
United States.   I. Title.
NA737.S525D68   1989   720'.92'4   88-43452
ISBN 0-8478-1035-6
ISBN 0-8478-1036-4 (pbk)

Designed by Abigail Sturges
Typeset by Rainsford Type, Danbury, CT
Printed and bound in Japan
Endpapers: Sketch by Shutze of house proposed for Thomas K.
Glenn on Sea Island, Georgia, 1938 (unbuilt)

This book has been produced in cooperation with, and with the
generous support of, the Atlanta Historical Society.

CONTENTS

ACKNOWLEDGEMENTS

I feel especially fortunate to be the first historian to receive access to the complete work of Philip Shutze. Shutze's career spanned some sixty years and included over 750 projects. It has taken four years of research to bring a sense of order to the diverse remnants of his rich production. During this period I received the support and assistance of many individuals and organizations. First I want to thank Louise Allen and Anne Carr for their keen interest in the realization of this book. Without their generous enthusiasm and deep appreciation of Shutze's architecture, which they had developed through discussions with him, this book could not have attained its present character. Next I want to thank Bill Fash for providing me with the research time required to document Shutze's architecture properly.

Many individuals provided insight into Shutze's character, especially Scotty Pannell, Shutze's great niece; original clients and friends, including Mrs. Julian Hightower, Mrs. Ben Smith, and Mrs. Richard Courts. Beth Jones, Betty Simmons, Alvin Cates, Joseph Mayson, Mrs. Joseph Curtis, Mrs. Albert Thornwell, David Robinson, and Floyd McRae provided enormous assistance with individual projects. Shutze's colleagues M.O. Saggus, Bill Finch, Harry Dwoskin, and Athos Menaboni provided views of his work habits. Henry Hope Reed provided assistance of various forms, most especially the first research into Shutze's career. I want to thank James Grady for his discussions of Shutze, and for the initial research on Neel Reid. I want to thank Charles and Bill Hough for their insights and for providing access to their collection of William Hough's drawings, letters, and photographs. I want to thank Jean Reeves for her help in the research in Philadelphia.

The many departments of the Atlanta Historical Society provided research assistance in Shutze's many collections. I am especially grateful to Don Rooney, who cheerfully provided his personal knowledge of Shutze's collections, and Ann

Salter, Elaine Kirkland, Spencer Tunnell, Bill Hull, Nancy Lester, Susan Hodges, Bill Richards, Nancy Wight, and Franklin Garrett. I want to thank John Ott for his constant support and interest in the quality of this work. I want to thank Tim Hursley for his personal interest in photographically expressing the character of Shutze's architecture.

Many colleagues provided assistance during the project. I want to thank Robert Venturi for his thoughts on Shutze's architecture early in the research; Marco Frascari for his discussions of the Italian qualities of Shutze's work; Robert Craig for his detailed review at a critical phase in writing; Doug Allen for discussions on Italian gardens; and Frank Beckum for his personal knowledge of Shutze. I want to thank Richard Macri for his two years of research assistance, especially his development of a complete job list for the firm. Clay Ulmer's excellent skills as a delineator are greatly appreciated. James Mount and Bernard Dotson provided an initial opportunity for me to publish my ideas on the modern aspect of Shutze's work and they also gave support and direction.

I especially want to thank Jeffrey Plank for bringing his diverse knowledge of the eighteenth century and of architecture to the editing of the manuscript. With his assistance this manuscript took shape.

Two foundations provided the financial assistance that allowed the realization of this book. The Georgia Tech Foundation assisted in my archival research in Philadelphia, New York, and Washington, D.C. and provided the archival photography for the book. The Philip Shutze Fund of the Metropolitan Atlanta Community Foundation provided the color photography essential to the understanding of his sensitive attention to architectural coloration.

The American Academy in Rome and the Archives of American Art provided generous assistance in researching their collections.

I especially thank David Morton of Rizzoli International for his personal interest in Shutze's architecture and his untiring assistance in realizing this book.

I thank my husband, Geddes, for sharing his reflections on design and his personal knowledge of Shutze. Finally, I thank my children, Meredith and Geddes, and my friend, Daisey Clark, for happily supporting my pursuit of this lengthy project.

Elizabeth Meredith Dowling

vii

PREFACE

Henry Hope Reed

In the triumphant age of American architecture when the classical reigned, more than one city was able to reward a talented native son. We think of Horace Trumbauer in Philadelphia, of David Adler on Chicago's North Shore, and of Arthur Brown, Jr., of San Francisco. These men raised their cities to the noble level of the grand tradition, and yet they have received slight recognition beyond those cities. Such a man was Philip Trammell Shutze. He placed Atlanta on the map of America's great classical architecture.

It was my good fortune to know Philip in the last years of his long life. At the urging of H. Strafford Bryant, an editor at W.W. Norton & Company, I went to Atlanta to see the work. The result was an article, "America's Greatest Living Classical Architect: Philip Trammell Shutze of Atlanta, Georgia," published in 1977 in *Classical America IV*. In giving him the accolade it would have seemed at first that I indulged in bravura. Actually, it was a statement of fact.

Then, there followed in 1979 the exhibition "Georgian Splendor: The Work of Philip Trammell Shutze of Atlanta." Organized by the Atlanta Historical Society and Classical America, it was held in Low Library at Columbia University on the initiative of the Avery Librarian, Adolph Placzek. It was Columbia's belated honoring of one of its outstanding students. Two years later the School of Architecture of the University of Texas and Classical America sponsored a conference and exhibition in Austin: "The Classical Tradition: The Wave of the Future." Philip's work was the core of the exhibition.

Finally, in 1982, the accolade was underscored when Classical America gave its first Arthur Ross Award in architecture to Philip, which was greeted by cheers at the ceremony.

What was particularly gratifying on that occasion was that Brooke Astor (Mrs. Vincent Astor), who presented the award, had long recognized Philip's worth. In 1949, as an editor of *House and Garden*, she had singled him out as superior. In so doing, she was the first to give the great architect national recognition. What is more, in her autobiography, *Footprints*, published in 1980, she recalled the strong impression Philip's work had made on her.

It was a privilege for me to follow him about in Atlanta. Inevitably I was rewarded in many ways. Of course, we shared disdain for modern art. With Philip, the disdain was not just for the practitioners but for the apologists, particularly in the academic world. What he could not get over was the extent of the abysmal ignorance of the art historian, the consequence of the abandonment of the classical.

We soon turned to the wonders of the grand tradition, Italian branch. His knowledge was extraordinary, as we can gather from the illustrations in this biography. He drew and measured the best our Mediterranean heritage has to offer. Little wonder that he could, with perfect ease, take inspiration from the Pantheon in his great banking hall for the Citizens and Southern Bank. Or adopt the cascade of Rome's Villa Corsini for the garden of Swan House. It is hardly surprising that he brushed off the modern movement as the aberration of the age and Frank Lloyd Wright as its chief *buffone* (adopting the Italian). For Philip observed the sweep of Western civilization from the brow of Rome's Capitoline Hill.

Yet he freely drew on Georgia's classical heritage, as we know from the Fulton County Medical Society building. In this he was not unlike Ogden Codman, Jr., of Boston who, while absorbed in the French and English 18th century, would turn to the New England architecture of the late colonial and the young republic.

Both men, it should be noted, thrust aside much of the 19th century architecture. They faulted particularly what might be termed the *Beaux Arts* approach. That is to say, an architecture where the plan dictated the design and the mixing of styles. Both men held to an older tradition, in Philip's case, to the Italian Renaissance, more especially the Roman Renaissance, which Edith Wharton in her *Italian Villas and Their Gardens* declared the mainspring of the classical of her day.

With his robust convictions in matters of art, we may well ask ourselves why he was not better known in the heyday of his practice. Admittedly, in those decades there was not the driving self-promotion by architects that is so much a part of our time. Still, one had to step forward to become known. That was simply not part of Philip. For him life was architecture, along with family, friends, growing camellias and, later in life, collecting Chinese export porcelain. Such was his shyness that, in 1926, an uncle active in business remonstrated with the firm of Hentz, Reid and Adler, where Philip was working, pointing out to the principals that his great skill as chief designer was deserving of a partnership. Philip became a partner.

Now that he is no longer with us, it is most fitting that the Atlanta Historical Society, proud owner of Swan House, Philip's best known work, should encourage Mrs. Dowling's biography. The Society is fulfilling one of its highest responsibilities in doing so, telling the world: We too can boast of a great American architect. Join us in studying the work of a citizen of Atlanta who has a lesson for all who care about the arts in America.

New York, 1988

INTRODUCTION

Vincent Scully

This book is a useful addition to those revisionist studies that are permitting us to assess more aspects of recent architectural history than most of us were prepared to do a generation ago. But there is no doubt that writing about P. T. Shutze raises some problems for an old modernist like myself. So many modern architects had Big Ideas, while Mr. Shutze had almost none. True enough, the work of all too many modernists was often architecturally primitivistic and urbanistically destructive, as Mr. Shutze's never was. Nor, in all justice, did Shutze pretend to theoretical interests he did not really possess, as so many of the modernists *pro forma* felt it necessary to do. But the very pretensions of the modernists, not to say the critical tangles in which they often involved themselves, made them interesting, willy-nilly, in all kinds of eccentric ways, perhaps unfortunately so. Mr. Shutze has to depend solely upon his architectural work. That is probably as it should be.

How good was that work? The answer has to be that it was sometimes very good indeed. The interior of the Citizens and Southern National Bank in Atlanta, for example, is startlingly grand. Its derivation is no less significant. It took shape out of no tormented linguistic theory, like those passing for history in so many architectural schools today—not out of the theory but out of Shutze's measurements of the details of the Pantheon itself. These were made while Shutze was a student at the American Academy in Rome, where he and his chums, teetering unathletically on the top rungs of unconvincing ladders, applied their rulers to the blasted leaves of the great ruined Corinthian capitals high in the air. Shutze did the same thing at the tip of Trajan's Column, one hundred Roman feet up: an aesthete with guts, obviously.

Mr. Shutze also did something else that was common practice in his generation but which very few modern architects were to do: he visited and studied gardens, especially the haunted classical-romantic gardens of Renaissance and baroque Italy, and he took them seriously. So he came back to Georgia and designed such gardens in close association with the country houses they served. Hence the garden traditions of Bramante, Pirro Ligorio, Vignola, and of Lutyens and Gertrude Jekyll as well, were still alive in Shutze, and they served in his work to connect the natural and the man-made in an eloquent and civilized discourse. Again, it is interesting that international-style modern architecture never developed a clear garden type of its own, despite the pictorial curlicues of Roberto Burle Marx and a few early experiments in a rather restricted cubist genre. The reason for that lack must lie partly in the word "cubism" itself—meaning that the deepest aesthetic of the international style was shaped by abstract modern painting rather than by those Renaissance and baroque architectural traditions that were literally based on the relationship between the man-made and the natural in the shaped space of the landscape itself. Hence modern country houses were set by preference either in untouched nature or in some diluted variation of the picturesque garden, which was the closest to seeming to be nature's mirror, and almost never in the classic garden. This was so, one supposes, because the classic garden had been so integral a part of the European urbanistic tradition, which the international style had so categorically renounced.

Yet, despite their many virtues, Shutze's country houses may sometimes seem rather blandly rich or weakly decorative to contemporary eyes. Are they so? Perhaps yes, but clearly no more so than any number of similar buildings by international-style architects. But in fact there is, I think, something a little soft and smug, a little untested about them. Perhaps Shutze learned his lessons in Italy well enough but those at home not nearly so well—or, at least, since he certainly knew the forms of the southern vernacular, not critically enough. Mrs. Dowling does not entirely agree with this, and shows us how Shutze's work does indeed seem to develop chronologically toward a more Americanized style in three stylistic phases: Italian baroque, English Regency, and, more or less finally, American Georgian. Still, his buildings throughout do seem to lack that wonderful tension between common vernacular traditions and rhetorical classical ideals that endows Jefferson's buildings with so much of their vitality, and which Robert Venturi has exploited so wittily in recent years. In consequence, despite its undoubted command of Renaissance scale and detail in particular, its often powerful sculptural presence, and the deeply rhythmic movement it can sometimes embody, there may seem to be something too suave and easy about Shutze's buildings. As Mrs. Dowling points out, the twentieth century simply never bothered Shutze; he ignored it.

True enough, it might be that this view is only a projection of our generation's taste for ambiguity—as if, in 1988, we needed some record of struggle, of imperfection, in order to believe wholeheartedly in any work of art. What we do like to see, certainly, is an awareness of alternatives and some conception of the ironic contraditions of modern life. Whatever the case, Shutze's work doesn't embody any of that at all. Hence it lacks the great contradictions that Lutyens, for example, was able to embody in his buildings, so endowing the classical language with a new particularity and vitality, as all the greatest classical architects have been able to do. Shutze's work, on the other hand, though it is among the very little that can stand comparison with Lutyens, is always close to its sources. His most renowned country houses clearly glory in being correctly "foreign," not local at all, and they lack any sense of the vital ambiguity of their situation, though Mrs. Dowling feels that the landscape of Atlanta is similar to that of the hillier parts of the Veneto, and therefore appropriate for Shutze's Italianate villa forms. She feels, too, that they are an image of the South's lost grandeur, with something touching in their snobbishness and their intimations of decay. This may be so, but Shutze seems always to be laying claim to somewhere else, even if only as far afield as Virginia, and even the incomparable Greek Revival of every little Georgia town from Savannah to Athens and Columbus is apparently too much like home for him.

That, too, may be a bit unfair to Shutze. The record of this book shows that he could also design very good vernacular buildings, especially in the "Brick Home" genre of his native South as a whole. Even these may look all too lush to Yankee eyes, but it is a fact that any number of architects throughout the South were doing spectacularly good work in that traditional mode right up until only a couple of decades ago. Indeed, from Memphis to Charleston and Baltimore to Mobile, many such architects came very close to surviving modernism and emerging as heroes in a post-modern architectural world that has not yet learned to do their stuff nearly so well as they could do it themselves. Shutze almost made it and, as Mrs. Dowling tells us, he lived long enough at least to see the modernism he had always hated roundly reviled in the criticism of the post-modern era.

Does this mean that the modern architects and critics had always been wrong and that Shutze and Classical America had always been right? It is true that Mrs. Dowling shows us a Shutze whose best work is far beyond the norm for Classical America, yet, perhaps stubbornly, one still feels reservations. Modernism's sins were legion, but some of them were surely splendid too, bold and stirring in ways Shutze could never be. Mrs. Dowling is to be commended, I think, for trying to touch upon some of those points, beyond which a few further comments about the American Academy in Rome might not be out of place. Shutze in his era at the Academy measured the surviving Roman details and reconstructed them. So did Louis I. Kahn, in his time during the 'fifties. He, inspired by the great classicist, the late Frank E. Brown, who was also profoundly modernist in his approach, tried to rebuild the ruins themselves, so dealing somehow with a primitive classicism, one which suggests crude new beginnings, even a magical rebirth of the bare bones of the old. Clearly, much was lost, and the classical language was unnecessarily reduced and primitivized thereby. But there was a violent power and a kind of knightly grandeur in Kahn's work that is missing from Shutze's and which remains, despite everything, somehow courageous, austere, moving, and terrible.

There can be no doubt, nevertheless, that our taste for the primitive has helped ruin our cities, which are what architecture is all about. Architecture cannot always be "beginning"; most of the time it has to be "continuing," instead. Architects like Venturi can deal with that essential condition in ways that stir our intelligence no less than our empathetic response. Shutze could not quite do that, but with what total control of their idiom the Italianate façades surge forward in his work; how, deep in Georgia, the strange, lost, classic gardens yearn.

New Haven, 1988

AMERICAN CLASSICIST

THE ARCHITECTURE OF
PHILIP TRAMMELL SHUTZE

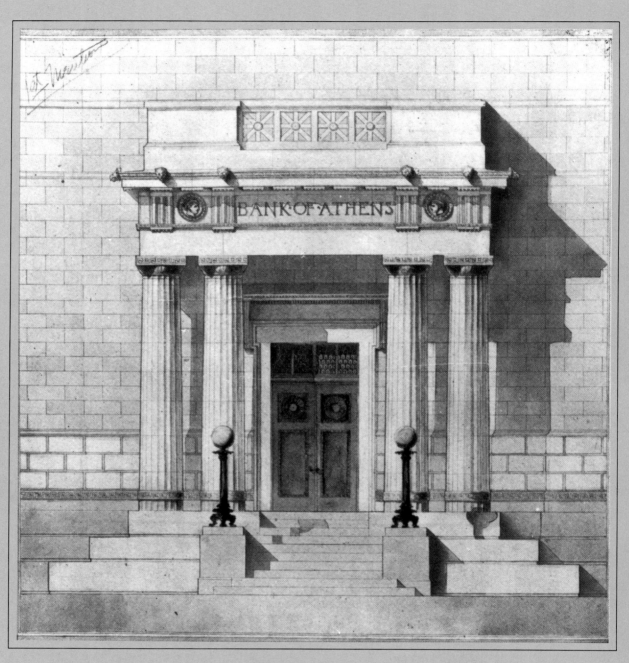

*1. A bank entrance designed by Shutze
during his sophomore year at Georgia Tech,
1909–10.*

I
EDUCATION AND PROFESSIONAL PREPARATION

2. Shutze with sketchbook and pencils above the Piazza Venezia in Rome, ca. 1917. Trajan's Column appears in the background

Philip Trammell Shutze was, by breeding and temperament, a product of the South. Yet through education and travel, his view of the world expanded beyond the provincialism of his early years, and his exceptional abilities flourished in the sophisticated atmosphere to which his education brought him. Southern gentility and continental elegance surfaced in Shutze's professional practice; he introduced to his native South a refinement of design unmatched since the era of cultured coastal life in Savannah and Charleston in the late eighteenth and early nineteenth centuries.

I

Philip Shutze was born on 18 August 1890 in Columbus, Georgia, to a family of comfortable means. Located on the Chattahoochee River, Columbus had recovered with surprising rapidity from the total devastation of its economic and political base at the end of the Civil War and by the last quarter of the century it prospered as a railroad and textile center.[1] The Chattahoochee River then served as an important trading connection to the Gulf of Mexico. Four riverboat companies operated from Columbus and six railroads converged on the city; it was an active commercial center with a population of approximately 17,000, and its architectural setting included several fine buildings, most of which were Renaissance inspired designs.[2]

Shutze's large extended family, including his paternal grandparents Mary A. Trammell and Daniel C. Schutze, who had emigrated from Bavaria to New York City in 1854, lived in and around Columbus. Lazarus Strauss, a family friend and neighbor from Germany, convinced Daniel Schutze to move to the small town of Talbotton, Georgia, where Strauss owned a mercantile business. From 1855 to 1865 Daniel Schutze taught music at various women's colleges, but when he lost all of his property at the end of the Civil War, his wife's family convinced him to join them in the family grocery business.[3] Shutze's father, also named Philip Trammell Shutze, was born in Greenville, Georgia, on 17 February 1861. The eldest of eight children, he apparently did not share his father's artistic inclinations, and after completing his high school education, he trained as a bookkeeper and bank cashier. He met and married Sallie Lee Erwin in West Point, Georgia, and they moved back to Columbus to raise their three children.

On 16 January 1900, while working for the Third National Bank, Shutze's father was shot and instantly killed by a deranged bank employee. The family's

3. *A Theater — Shutze's senior thesis at Georgia Tech, 1911–12.*

comfortable existence immediately deteriorated. His mother moved the children, Faye, Thomas, and Philip, closer to relatives, first to Atlanta and then to West Point, his mother's childhood home, where Shutze received his high school education. In 1908 he graduated as valedictorian from public high school, and he won a scholarship to attend the Georgia School of Technology in Atlanta. The family returned to Atlanta so that they could be with Philip during his studies at Georgia Tech.

In choosing to study architecture, Shutze found an acceptable outlet for his artistic talent in a stable and responsible professional field. The School of Architecture had opened in 1908, and by 1910 it was headed by Francis Palmer Smith, a recent graduate of the University of Pennsylvania. At Pennsylvania, Smith had studied with the renowned French architect and critic Paul Cret, and at Georgia Tech Smith developed an architectural program typical of the period, an Americanized version of the instructional system at the Ecole des Beaux-Arts. In their first year the students learned drafting skills, shades and shadows, and perspective, and in their sophomore year they designed small buildings. The curriculum emphasized history, freehand drawing, rendering, and design, and Shutze excelled in each area (*figures 1, 3*).

In the summer of 1911, Shutze, like all serious American architectural students of his time, made an architectural pilgrimage to Western Europe. His letters brim with the youthful excitement of discovering the greater world; arriving in Paris he wrote:

> We rolled into Paris—my dear mother, at midnight—yes 12 o'clock at night—, us—two strangers—ignorant—unsophisticated mortals in the second largest city in the world—in the Gare du Nord and not a soul did we know. We were 8 hours in making the little journey from Antwerp to Paris. Think of it—no distance whatever. Only a matter of $3.26 cents.

3

We started out to walk around and see Paris just for novelties' [sic] sake. We had our Baedeckers along and there was no danger of our getting ourselves misplaced. We walked from the Gare du Nord down to Latin Quarter—Tuileries—Eifel [sic]—Trocadero—Place d'Etoile—oh—I can't begin to name the places—and first thing we knew it was broad daylight—We didn't go to bed all that day—but walked around looked—ate every once in a while—rested our weary bones here and there—Mama—when afternoon came we were nearly dead. . . . [4]

Mama—I am having the times of my life—I am charmed—everything here just breathes of art—and beauty—Never dreamed of such architecture, sculpture and painting. [5]

This passage, with its tender regard for his distant mother's concern and its enthusiasm for the immediacy of a sophisticated culture, perfectly contrasts Shutze's provincial origins with his nascent sensibilities. Throughout his years at Georgia Tech, Shutze supported himself by working for the architectural firm of Hentz and Reid, and after graduation, he continued to work for the firm whenever he lived in Atlanta. In this initial period, he contributed to several significant projects, including the first East Lake Country Club of 1914, designed in an early English Renaissance style (*figure* 8). Shutze drew details for the formal rooms rendered appropriately in dark carved woodwork.

Neel Reid and especially Hal Hentz also participated in the training of students at Georgia Tech. The example of Reid and Hentz, who had both studied at Columbia University and for a brief period at the Ecole des Beaux-Arts, significantly influenced Shutze's decision to pursue extensive academic training. [6] In 1912, Shutze graduated with honors from Georgia Tech and, at the urging of his employers, enrolled with a scholarship in the architectural program at Columbia, then one of the finest in the country. William R. Ware, who had founded the first American program in architectural education at the Massachusetts Institute of Technology in 1868, had established Columbia's School of Architecture in 1881. When Shutze arrived at Columbia in the fall, a new director, Austin Willard Lord (1860–1922), and a new building, Avery Hall, greeted the students. For the first time in the school's history, all of the ateliers and the Avery Library were consolidated in a single building. A practicing architect, Lord was selected to strengthen the professional character of the school and to improve the design

4

5

GYMNASIVM · ON · A · LAKE · SHORE

4. A Gymnasium on
a Lakeshore, Shutze's
thesis at Columbia
University, 1913,
plan.
5. Elevation.

courses. A contemporary account indicates the new emphasis on design that Shutze encountered:

> Student work in design must be passed not only by these three critics in their field, but also by three other professors in their special branches; Professor Hamlin for historical accuracy; Professor Sherman for correctness in shades, shadows and perspective; Professor Warren for the use of materials of construction and for structural stability and reliability. It is the intention of the staff to develop by this means of cooperation a course in design of unparalleled scope, encouraging the student to consider his effort from every angle of vision and to regard it as the crowning witness of his ability, his maximum of efficiency.[7]

A. D. F. Hamlin was considered one of America's foremost historians and his son, Talbot Hamlin, who was to achieve comparable fame as a historian, was a member of Shutze's class.

The evidence of Shutze's projects, some of which were published in the *Annual of the School of Architecture*, indicates that the Columbia program was more rigorous and more sophisticated than the one he had completed at Georgia Tech. His Columbia thesis, a gymnasium on a lakeshore, is an immense scheme based on the Baths of Caracalla in Rome (*figures 4, 5*). His solution is an exceptionally refined composition; it displays his mastery of French *axe*, *enfilade*, delicate *poché* and *entourage* employed on a monumental scale.[8] The gymnasium is a much more involved bulding type than the ones he had worked with at Georgia Tech. It allowed him to compose a variety of shaped interior spaces and to consider the subtleties of relating complex interior to exterior spaces.

Shutze and Talbot Hamlin each received third place medals for an *esquisse-esquisse* titled "A Monument to Cuban Independence" (*figures 6, 7*). Although the projects were judged equals, Shutze used light and dark rendered areas to focus compositional attention, whereas Hamlin attended so minutely to details that he sacrificed compositional unity and power.

After he graduated from Columbia in 1913 with a second Bachelor of Architecture degree, Shutze returned to Atlanta to work once again for Hentz and Reid, and to serve as an instructor in the Department of Architecture at Georgia Tech. From 1913 to 1915, Shutze worked on a number of commissions including a manorial home for Fuller Callaway in La Grange, Georgia, and the East Lake

6

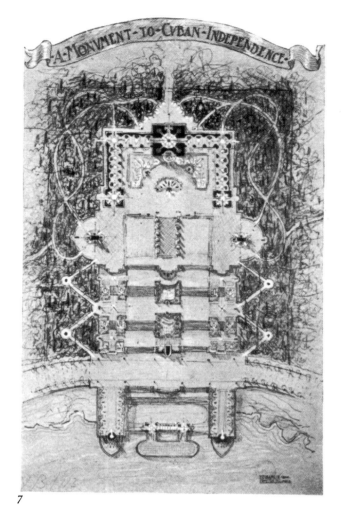

7

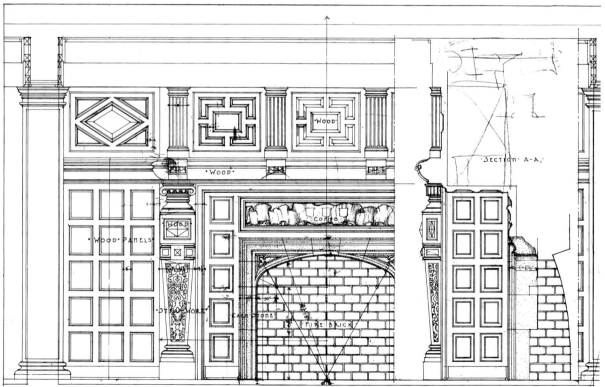

8

6. A monument to
Cuban Independence,
Shutze's third-place-
medal esquisse-
esquisse, Columbia
University, 1912–13.
7. Talbot Hamlin also
received a third-place
medal for the same
problem.

8. Details of the living
room of the East Lake
Country Club in
Atlanta, drawn by
Shutze in 1914.

9

9. *Decoration of an Island Commemorating its Purchase, Shutze's Rome Prize, 1915, sponsored by the American Academy in Rome,* esquisse.
10. *Plan.*
11. *Elevation.*

10

THE DECORATION OF AN ISLAND COMMEMORATING ITS PVRCHASE

11

Country Club in Atlanta. He made drawings of the public rooms of the 1914 club using two generic models—the early English baronial house and the Scottish golf clubhouse. Stone and wood details, such as the wood paneled walls and the fireplace with its double centered opening surmounted by swirling masonry pennants, created an appropriate masculine environment for the club's membership.

In 1915 Shutze entered the competition for the Rome Prize. This architectural award was considered the finest in an era of numerous significant student prizes. It was worth $3,000 for three years of study and travel in Italy; by contrast, the Paris Prize, its nearest rival, brought $2,500 for two-and-a-half years' study at the Ecole. Shutze had seen the Rome Prize competition entries while studying at Columbia, and in 1914 a former Georgia Tech classmate, W. Pope Barney, received an honorable mention. Barney and all the other 1914 winners were then students at the University of Pennsylvania, and this impressive showing brought Pennsylvania great attention. His former classmate's success and the close ties with Pennsylvania of his former teacher Francis Palmer Smith no doubt drew Shutze into the competition.

The 1915 problem, "The Decoration of an Island Commemorating its Purchase," consisted of four major elements—a commemorative monument, an open-air theater, formal gardens, and a great bridge. Beyond these requirements, the program encouraged students to display their compositional abilities freely. The competition was presented in two stages, French equivalents of which were the *esquisse* and the *projet rendu*.[10] Shutze entered the first stage of the competition under the supervision of the Department of Architecture at Georgia Tech and, at the end of the fourteen-hour problem, he produced an exceptional design (*figure 9*). The *Atlanta Constitution* reported his initial success: "From the scores of entries throughout the country, the best four designs were selected by the American Academy in Rome jury in New York. Those who saw Mr. Shutze's drawing here [Atlanta] were not surprised when it was learned that he had secured one of the four coveted places as it showed a firm grasp of the problem and was remarkable in its presentation."[11] These four were then asked to develop their initial concepts.

Shutze's *esquisse* established the location of the major elements, defined the shape of his imaginary island, and determined the proportions of the bridge entering the island. Shutze rendered his design dramatically with light and dark

9

entourage and, in the custom of the day, left the individual elements sufficiently indistinct to allow for further adjustments.

Shutze developed his finished scheme in an atelier at Columbia University, and through its dramatic organization and rendered form (*figures 10, 11*), it communicated a stirring emotionalism that was to become a hallmark of his professional work. Once again the *Constitution* lauded his success: "The four logists were allowed six weeks in which to restudy their solutions and make the final drawings at a large scale in water color. The only word of criticism regarding the designs that has been heard came from William R. Meade [sic], president of the Academy, who said that Mr. Shutze's design was the finest piece of student work he had ever seen!"[12] To create striking focus in this finished design, Shutze placed the major gathering point, the open-air theater, at the lower end of the island and led the eye up to a monumental obelisk on the island's crest by means of the theater's semicircular seating pattern and rising tiers of steps and water cascades. Even in this early work, Shutze displayed his extraordinary capacity for relating details to masses and his impressive control of the design principles of French composition.

He had competed without success for the Paris Prize when he was at Columbia, but Shutze's success in the Rome Prize and his subsequent period of study in Italy permanently shaped his future and established his identity as a designer. Shutze received a first medal in the 1912–13 Paris Prize, and if he had won the Paris Prize instead of the Rome Prize and studied in Paris rather than Rome, as American students typically did, his experiences, education, and probably his professional career would have been entirely different. The architecture programs at Georgia Tech and Columbia were both patterned after the French system, and additional years in Paris with further intensive atelier training in competitions would have merely sharpened a particular design approach that his Rome Prize entry demonstrated he had already mastered. Whether he was aware of the differences or not, his experience in Rome was formulated to be a different type of training from that of Paris.

In the architectural literature of the early 1900s, proponents of Paris and Rome debated the relative merits of these educational programs. One writer summarized the difference this way: "Rome teaches what to do, Paris how to do it."[13] With the exception of one collaborative problem each year, teamwork replaced competition at the American Academy; students assisted one another in measuring ornamental details, facades, garden plans, and architectural remains. The ultimate goal of the brightest French students at the Ecole was to win their own Grand Prix de Rome—a point not overlooked by proponents of the American Academy.

In 1912, Charles Henry Cheney described the freedom of research that Rome offered to students and the Academy's distinctive plan of education:

> Designed for mature men, it is not the purpose of the Academy to offer definite courses of instruction. It is not a school in the sense of the Ecole des Beaux-Arts in Paris, for instance. It is planned essentially for the man approaching thirty years of age, fully developed in technique and with some years of practical experience in his profession. He must already be trained in what to look for—to see possibilities as well as actualities—and he should be able to put down easily what he sees and thinks. Only thus equipped can he derive the greatest benefit of his sojourn there; it may well be said that "the more a man takes with him to Rome the more he will bring back." Coming after years of projects and the steady grind of preparatory work, this three-year period offers the artist a breathing spell to "find" himself, and at the same time the opportunity to acquire culture and taste in the most inspiring environment the world possesses.[14]

Tempering his remarks on the French system, Cheney observed that studying classical architecture gave an architect a balanced approach to design: "One of the greatest things gained from the French system of training, is opposition to copying and to too much formalism. Keeping this in mind a thorough knowledge of the classic forms is only a proper steadying influence to the strong modern tendency to originality, which, untutored, generally has ended only in the bizarre."[15]

Shutze sailed for Europe in the fall of 1915 to begin the most formative period of his life—five years of study, travel, and war service that would shape his great talent into that of, perhaps, the finest American classicist of the twentieth century. At the Academy, he developed a design approach that deviated from the widely accepted values and techniques of Beaux-Arts classicism, and during his professional career he never referred to the French planning concepts taught at Georgia Tech and Columbia; frequently he expressed his distaste for the Ecole.

12. The American Academy in Rome, photo, ca. 1912.

II

In 1915, the Academy had recently moved to the new quarters designed by McKim, Mead, and White (*figure 12*) adjacent to the Villa Aurelia. Students who had lived in both the old and the new buildings resented the move because the new one had not aged enough and was too shiny and unsympathetic to the timeworn quality they appreciated so much in Rome. William Hough, the Fellow in Architecture for 1914, expresses this attitude in a letter to his aunt:

> The other day I visited one of the Roman villas—built in the 16th century. Age of course had mellowed everything so that the whole place had a quiet, dignified air—elegant enough to befit a rich nobleman—yet so restrained that even I felt as if it could be a "home." And while there, I couldn't help but compare it or rather contrast it with our new Academy building where we live—built by American millionaires, and kept up in the spirit that all Europeans believe America as a whole possesses. We have fine equipment and are made very comfortable, yet the ostentatious newness of our "home" does seem out of place here in Italy, where everything Italian seems hallowed with age and subdued by the experience of generations. . . . [T]he Italian villa, though well kept and passably clean, has a musty dusty air about it which seems to tie it all in with Mother Earth—and you feel like a real human being in it instead of an artificial hot-house variety of the species.[16]

Still, contrast of new construction with authentic classical buildings may have finely attuned the Academy fellows to the characteristics of architectural age, which Shutze would later recreate so accurately in Atlanta. Shutze particularly noticed the weathering of the buildings he visited. Centuries of rain and brilliant sun had smoothed refinements in the stucco work of the old Italian buildings, and it was these effects and subtle signs of age rather than the perfect detailing of the new Academy building that Shutze would later emulate in his new buildings in Atlanta. The new location of the American Academy was more central to the city, however, and its scenic vistas atop Rome's highest point within the city walls, the Janiculum, offered spectacular views of the city below.

Shutze left little information about his tenure in Italy; only a few letters written during his five years abroad remain. An extraordinary record of the period has survived from Allyn Cox, the 1916 American Academy Fellow in Painting. A devoted correspondent, Cox wrote once a week to his family, which included his father, the well-known muralist Kenyon Cox. Cox mentions Shutze frequently, and his letters tell much about attitudes and life at the Academy during the difficult years of World War I.

According to Cox, the two students shared a love of the Italian baroque which caused some distress among other Academy students who preferred the High Renaissance. Geoffrey Scott, a personal friend of Cox, shared an interest in the baroque and frequented Rome after the publication in 1914 of his book *The Architecture of Humanism.*[18] In one letter, Cox recorded that Scott had discussed coming to America after the war ended and that he had wondered whether Americans would like baroque villas.[19] Although Scott did not pursue this thought, Shutze did, and within four years he had begun to design baroque projects on the hilly Atlanta landscape for enthusiastic clients.

Cox knew that the ambience of Italy and its influence on the Academy differed from the students' educational experiences in the United States. He found the environment of Rome at once stimulating and suffocating, and he speculated that too much good work surrounding a person could produce a feeling that everything had already been done: "I am afraid of turning into a sweet gentle connoisseur person of refined tastes."[20] Apparently this feeling was not uncommon among Academy students. In a letter to his father in April 1917, Cox wrote: "There is an ancient and elaborate tradition in the art of doing as little as possible as neatly and elegantly as possible."[21] Shutze later remarked that one project a year was politely suggested, but this urbane attitude belies the rigor of the Academy program; students were assigned fewer projects, but they were expected to put far

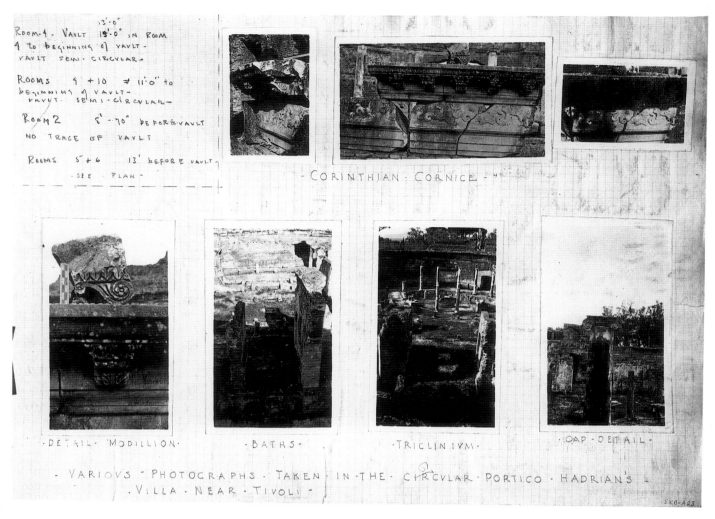

ROOM·4· VAVLT 13'-0" 15'-0" IN ROOM
4 to beginning of VAVLT·
VAVLT SEMI· CIRCVLAR·

ROOMS 9 +10 ≠ 11'·0" to
beginning of VAVLT·
VAVLT· SEMI·CIRCVLAR·

ROOM 2   8'·-10" BEFORE VAVLT
NO TRACE OF VAVLT

ROOMS 5 + 6   13' BEFORE VAVLT·
·SEE· PLAN·

·CORINTHIAN· CORNICE·

·DETAIL· MODILLION·   ·BATHS·   ·TRICLINIVM·   ·CAP· DETAIL·

·VARIOVS· PHOTOGRAPHS· TAKEN· IN·THE· CIRCVLAR· PORTICO· HADRIAN'S·
·VILLA· NEAR· TIVOLI·

SKG-A23

13. A page from Shutze's Academy sketchbook with notes and photographs taken for his first restoration study.

14. Details of Villa Lante, Rome. A page from Shutze's Academy sketchbook, in which the plumb bob indicates the technique used for recording the depth of moldings.

15. Measured drawing of the Villa Lante, rendered in pencil on tracing paper (inset).

more effort and time into them. Results make it clear that Academy students converted considerable instruction into significant work.

Although World War I was being waged in France and Germany, it had little affect on the daily activities of Academy students who pursued their busy schedule of lectures, travel, and drawing. The director, Jesse Benedict Carter, and later Gorham Phillips Stevens, organized sketching trips in Rome and the surrounding countryside. One such trip took Shutze and other fellows to Pompeii. His first drawing sketchbook includes six pages of molding profiles, accompanied by small photographs of details and views, and notes arranged meticulously on the pages. Such focus on arrangement soon disappeared from his sketchbooks as he grew accustomed to his methods and as the purpose of the material grew more clear.

During Shutze's tenure, the Academy offered a loosely structured three-year program of study that required measured and rendered drawing each year. During the first year, students concentrated on ancient Rome; in the second, the Renaissance; and in the third, either antique or Renaissance subjects. Within a subject

14

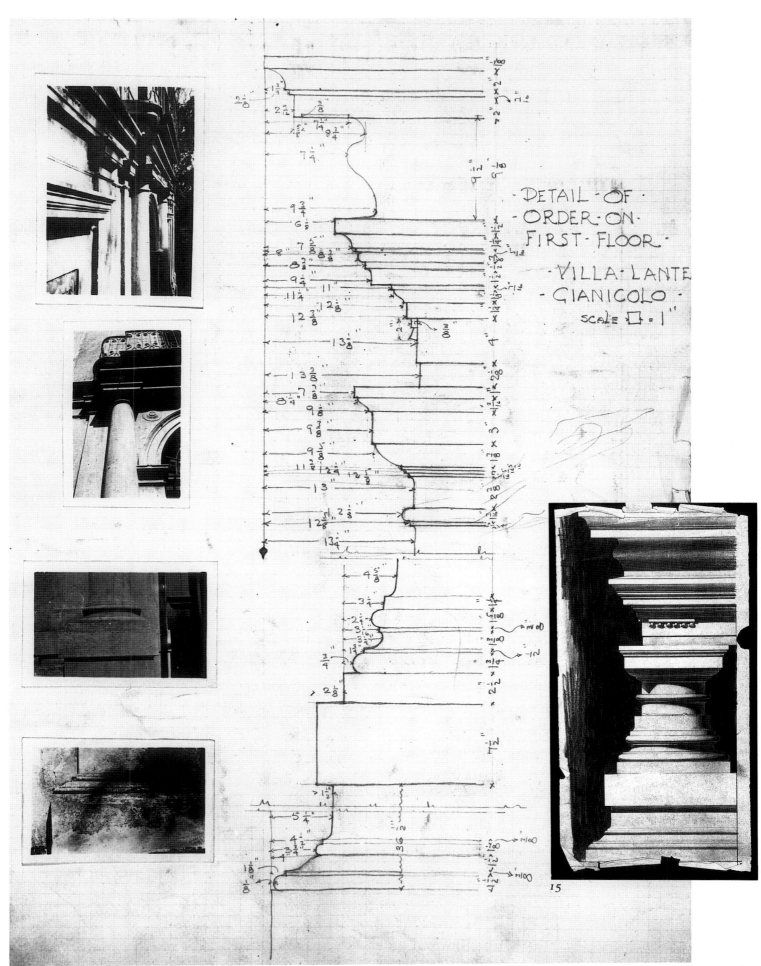

· DETAIL · OF ·
· ORDER · ON ·
FIRST · FLOOR ·

· VILLA · LANTE
· GIANICOLO ·

SCALE ☐ = 1"

15

category titled "general studies," students researched the proportions of building elements in the Academy's library and on location. In addition, the faculty lectured each year on Roman history, topography, and archaeology. The educational result, the trustees hoped, was the development of culture—a refinement overlooked in American and French education in the pursuit of technique.[22]

The measuring of buildings was the Academy's primary method of conveying to its fellows the subleties of classical architecture. In this laborious and sometimes dangerous activity, the fellows focused on details; they learned to appreciate the proportions and scale of architectural details, as well as the elements of classical ornamentation (*figure 14*). The Academy provided a financial allowance for "ladder hire" to all architecture and landscape architecture fellows to enable them to perform the acrobatic feats of measuring elements such as the column capitals of the Temple of Neptune, or Bernini's Colonnade at St. Peter's (*figures 17, 22*).[23] The fellows usually assisted one another in taking measurements and thereby studied far more buildings than the few that each finally rendered in painstaking fashion.

In 1917, Shutze and William Hough measured the Pantheon portico and interior details (*figures 18, 66–69*). Both Shutze's and Hough's Academy sketchbooks survive, each an oblong hardcover book of bound paper ruled with a grid of lines. The similarity of page layout for the Pantheon data along with photographs of the two taking measurements show how students worked together to record their information.[24] Photographs of this measuring trip show clearly the physical effort required.[25] Shutze was not the athlete Hough was (who had lettered in three sports at Pennsylvania). But Shutze's intellectual curiosity prompted him to pursue his art to dizzying heights. Even more daring than the Pantheon adventure was the students' assault upon Trajan's Column. Surviving photographs include Shutze at the base of the column recording information; others show Shutze and Hough at the top of the column, over 100 feet above the ground, suspended on a small, insubstantial platform (*figures 20, 21, 23*).

As Cox's correspondence attests, Shutze was attracted to the baroque, while most students were drawn to the High Renaissance; the subjects he selected for his measured restorations were therefore somewhat idiosyncratic. Except for his restoration of Hadrian's Circular Pavilion at Tivoli (A.D. 124), which in itself is an elaborate composition (*figures 24–27*), Shutze's studies all were of baroque subjects. Apparently he was attracted to the greater emotional and sensual nature of the baroque, with its curving surfaces, three-dimensional stacking of architectural elements, and its overall freedom from the self-imposed restraint of the Renaissance. This love of the baroque first blossomed in Italy, and it characterized his work throughout his career.

Hadrian's Circular Pavilion, Shutze's first restoration study, is a small but spatially complex design of curving and countercurving walls and peristyles. Its name derives from the circular plan of an exterior colonnade of forty Ionic columns that support a vaulted roof and an interior circular pavilion with variously shaped rooms framed about a centered fountain. This diminutive villa is surrounded by a water moat, hence its other name of "Island Villa."

Shutze's drawings show the pavilion restored to active life—peopled with Roman citizens lounging on chairs, bathing, or strolling. His imaginative recreation of Hadrian's villa decorated with draperies, furniture, wall murals, and statuary perhaps suggested a method for developing coordinated interiors. In his later professional design development drawings Shutze always included fully furnished and peopled interior sketches, perhaps to provide his clients with lessons in the decorative arts.

His other rendered subjects are Roman baroque: the fountain of the Tartarughe, and the facades of the Villa Spada, the Villa Lante, and Santa Maria della Pace. Each refined his interests in the plastic qualities of sixteenth- and seventeenth-century architecture. Shutze must have selected the Villa Spada and the Villa Lante to study scale, proportion, and detailing (*figures 28–30*). Each villa is approximately the same width and height, and each is approached by double curving stairs; the two are distinguished through their details. Stacked orders are used in one, and giant (two-story) orders in the other. Walls filled with details of equal emphasis are matched by plain walls, which focused attention on the central three-dimensional details. Shutze used these lessons in design later in his career.

Shutze did a measured study of Santa Maria della Pace in Rome to learn how to achieve a sensual orchestration of architectural form—complex intersections of curving three-dimensional surfaces, a projecting curved portico, curving wings, stacked orders, sculpture (*figures 31, 32*). Although Shutze designed projects of equal complexity, he never saw them realized. The Tartarughe Fountain represents numerous garden ornaments that Shutze measured and photographed (*figure 33*). These elements he also used on many occasions.

Following pages:
16. Shutze and Gorham Stevens on the ladder taking measurements of the Portico of Octavia, Rome, 1917.
17. Shutze and Raymond Kennedy measuring the Temple of Neptune, Rome, 1917.
18. Shutze and William Hough on the ladder measuring the portico of the Pantheon, Rome, 1917.
19. Raymond Kennedy serves as a six-foot scale figure in the Pantheon, Rome, 1917.
20. William Hough and Gorham Stevens measuring the entasis on the Column of Trajan, Rome, 1917.
21. Shutze and Raymond Kennedy making a rubbing of inscriptions on the base of Trajan's Column, Rome, 1917.
22. William Hough and another student measuring details of Bernini's colonnade, St. Peter's, Rome, 1917.
23. Shutze, William Hough, and Wilton measuring the capital of the Column of Trajan, approximately 125 ft. above the ground, Rome, 1917.

17

16

17

18

19

20

21

22

23

CIRCVLAR

MOAT

CHAMBER

MOAT

BRIDGES·ON·ROLLER

PORTICO

VESTIBVLE

TERRACE OF THE
GREEK AND LATIN LIBRARIES

A·RESTORATION·OF·
THE·CIRCVLAR·
PAVILION·AT·
HADRIAN'S·VILLA·
NEAR·TIVOLI·

PLAN·
·SCALE·IN·FEET·

FOVNTAIN

24

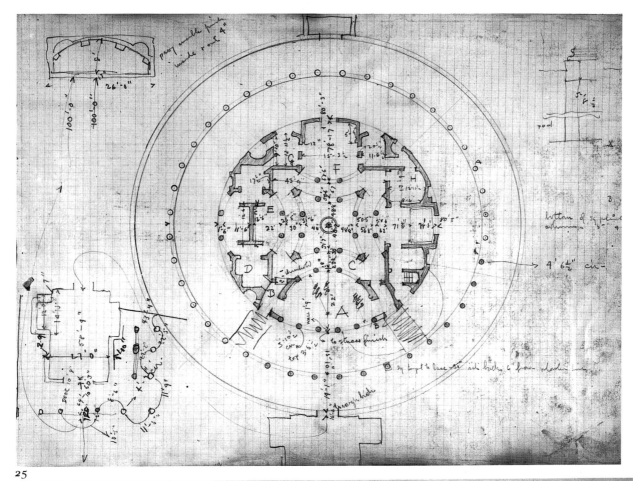

24. Circular Pavilion at Hadrian's Villa, Tivoli, restoration plan. Shutze's rendered restoration plan developed from his field measurements.
25. A page from Shutze's Academy sketchbook with notes and field measurements.
26. Section.
27. Rendered section.

25

26

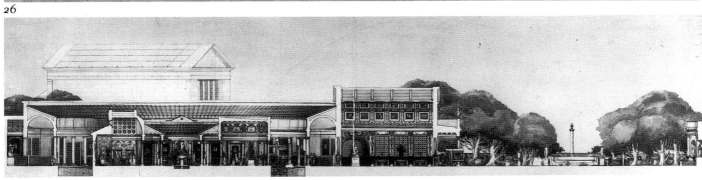

27

21

28

28. Villa Spada,
Rome, Shutze's
measured restoration
study.

29. Villa Lante,
Rome, Shutze's
measurements of a
baluster from his
Academy sketchbook.
30. Shutze's measured
restoration study of
the villa.

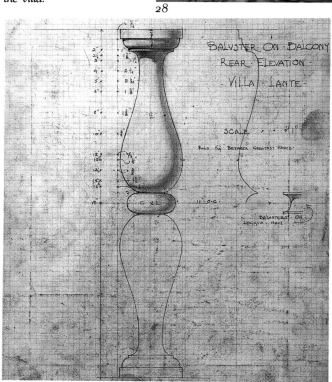

29

30

The American Institute of Architects (AIA) judged and awarded a prize for the one competitive project sanctioned in the Academy—the yearly collaborative. This unique competition demanded a solution that combined architecture, painting, and sculpture as equal contributions to the design; by necessity, groups of students learned to coordinate their efforts. Each year that Shutze participated in a collaborative, his team won the prize. His most interesting project, "A Monument to a Great General," was designed in 1920 with Cox and Thomas H. Jones, Fellow in Sculpture (*figure 34*). Inspired by the Pantheon, the domed circular temple focuses upon an apse that houses a statue of George Washington, Shutze's personal hero. The dome is surrounded by gesturing figures painted by Cox, and Jones sculpted the statue and the model itself. Shutze's customary study of precedent without slavish adherence to the studied object is already evident in this design.

His last major project of 1920 was another collaborative work and, in a sense, was a thesis statement of all that he had learned in the preceding years. With Jones and Edward Lawson, Fellow in Landscape Architecture, Shutze designed a new American ambassador's residence for a suburb of Rome. This baroque scheme embraced the hilly landscape with such authenticity that one could easily mistake it for another reconstruction project (*figures 35–37*). Conceptually the scheme creates a setting of formal grandeur appropriate to a head of state; Shutze developed it by elaborating the Italian villa model. He carefully orchestrated movement from entry drive to house to garden to heighten the experience of visiting the ambassador. Unlike the villas Shutze had studied, this casino, or residence, has two strikingly ornate baroque facades. The arrival facade is approached either by car on symmetrical curving ramps, or by foot on a double curving horseshoe stair. Inside, a grand staircase within a two-story covered cortile gives access to a suite of shaped rooms on the *piano nobile*, which opens to formal gardens. Shutze ornamented the garden with a series of events including a small domed building, a terrace of clipped box in patterns, and a garden theater and ilex and laurel tunnel similar to the elements Lawson and he had studied at the Villa Gori. Much of the spirit of the project would reappear in Atlanta projects, particularly the Calhoun residence on West Paces Ferry Road that was designed soon after his return to America.

Shutze never exhibited an interest in architectural theory. Georgia Tech,

31

31. Santa Maria della
Pace, Rome, Shutze's
measured restoration
study. His choice of
subject for detailed
study demonstrates his
interest in baroque
architecture.

32. Elevation and
plan. Freehand
drawings from a page
of Shutze's Academy
sketchbook.

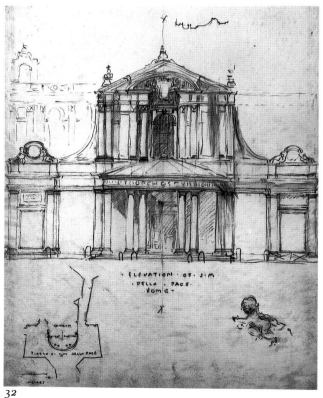

32

33

34

33. Tartarughe Fountain, Rome, Shutze's measured restoration study.

34. The American Institute of Architects' collaborative problem of 1920, winning solution designed by Shutze, Allyn Cox, and Thomas H. Jones, Fellows in architecture, painting, and sculpture.

35

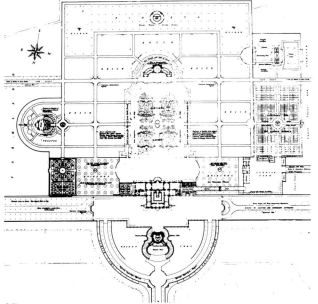

36

37

Columbia, and the Academy placed little emphasis on theory; Shutze wrote infrequently, and when he did, it was in a poetic, interpretative manner. The surviving examples of his writing indicate that he took enormous care in writing and rewriting passages. Written exploration of ideas appears to have been far more arduous for him than design. It is his built work which clearly indicates that Shutze wholeheartedly accepted classicism as the only basis for architectural design.

His most formative exposure to theoretical discussions of classicism occurred at the Academy. Shutze arrived in Italy the year following the publication of Scott's *Architecture of Humanism*. This book may have resolved any theoretical concerns Shutze had with architecture. His direct friendship with Scott cannot be confirmed, but there are many circumstantial connections. Scott often visited Rome and the Academy, and while working as librarian and secretary for Bernard Berenson, he met Allyn Cox, who frequently visited Berenson at the Villa I Tatti near Florence. As a proponent of classicism, Scott sought to categorize the criticism leveled by critics such as John Ruskin. Scott dismissed their criticism through examination of what he called fallacies: romantic, mechanical, ethical, and biological. Most of his discussion is aimed at the antithesis of classicism, the Gothic movement popular in the nineteenth century, but he also attacks iron and glass architecture. After rejecting all alternatives, Scott presents humanist architecture (another name for classicism) as the only appropriate style. He finds this architecture valuable because it developed from an interpretation of the human body in architectural terms. Not only do capitals and their shafts relate proportionately as human heads to their bodies, but our senses perceive buildings to swell, spring, stretch, sink, or soar, to be calm or restless. In reality, static buildings do none of these. Scott wrote that "the scientific perception of the world is forced upon us; the humanist perception of it is ours by right. The scientific method is intellectually and practically useful, but the naive, the anthropomorphic way which humanizes the world and interprets it by analogy with our own bodies and our own wills, is still the aesthetic way; it is the basis of poetry, and it is the foundation of architecture."[26]

Shutze's five years in Italy were not focused entirely upon the Academy. Rome had remained untouched by the horrors of World War I until late 1917, when the Academy closed and most students enlisted their services with the

American Red Cross in Italy. Jesse Carter, director of the Academy, previously had gone to the Italian front to arrange for his students to join an ambulance corps, but while organizing this unit he died of heatstroke. Gorham Stevens succeeded Carter as director, and his decision to enlist in the Red Cross prompted decisive action by his students.[28] Shutze was the first Academy student to follow him, but Cox and Hough found themselves in a typical dilemma. Both contemplated returning to America to enlist, but the dangers of a transatlantic voyage and a possible encounter with German U-boats made this a risky option; if they took it, they knew they immediately would be returned to Europe on the even more dangerous voyage of a troopship. Enlisting for Red Cross duty in Paris was an alternative, but since it was the one apparently pursued by most Americans in Europe, there were far more applicants than openings. Hough considered joining the "camouflage," whose work involved painting railroads, roads, and other strategic objects; however, as he wrote his family, "I doubt if my lines could be very straight with fireworks about."[29] The camouflage corps was also part of the regular army, to which Hough, a Quaker, objected.

The students' war activities varied more by chance than by choice or talent. Shutze served as a lieutenant in Ancona at a railroad station canteen that helped feed and clothe both Italian and Allied troops, and "emaciated, ragged, wet, cold, and hungry" ex-prisoners.[30] Hough served as a warehouse officer, and Cox moved about Italy establishing schools to instruct Italian women and young girls in the largely forgotten art of lacemaking, which, it was hoped, would make them economically self-sufficient after the war.[31] The fellows' war service lasted exactly one year from their enlistment in November 1917 until Armistice Day on 11 November 1918. Lucia and Alan Valentine's history of the Academy describes the joyous return of the fellows to their home in Rome:

> After the armistice of November 11, 1918, the Academy buildings were illuminated with every light that could be found. Thanksgiving that year was felt truly and deeply, if not solemnly. At dinner the twenty-three who were present included Charles Platt and Paul Manship, whom war services had brought to Rome. There was music, while live turkeys were paraded, gobbling excitedly, around the table: with each course a larger turkey appeared—or so the story goes. As the dessert appeared so did two doves, one with an American and the other with an Italian flag. They flew distractedly

over the endangered heads of the celebrants, as turkey and wine symbolized the thankfulness of Italy and America for the war's end.[32]

After his discharge from Red Cross service, Shutze returned to the Academy to continue his fellowship, but in the spring of 1919, he learned that his mother, Sallie Lee Shutze, was gravely ill and he immediately sailed to America. After she died, Shutze remained in Atlanta until the Academy officially reopened in the fall of 1919.

While in Atlanta, he worked for his former employers, now Hentz, Reid and Adler, and participated in the design of several projects, the foremost of which was the Howard Theatre (now demolished). The only surviving study for the Howard Theatre facade (*figure 45*) differs markedly from the final design (*figure 38*). The facade was reworked with unfortunate results after Shutze's departure for Italy, and the strength of his composition was diminished. The interior, however, maintained a consistently baroque grandeur (*figures 39, 40*). Clusters of Corinthian pilasters and attached columns rendered in marbleized plaster flanked the central stage. Above the proscenium, reclining nude figures cradled an elaborate cartouche. And, on either side of the proscenium, a plaster cartouche and scrolls engraved in Latin *Anno domini mille nongenti-et-viginti* (indicating the year of construction) surmounted matching theater boxes.[33]

In the fall of 1919 Shutze returned to Rome on what was termed a suspended fellowship.[34] During this final year, he produced both the collaborative problem, which fully titled was "A room in a public building which is suitable for a statue of a great general," and his thesis project for a new American ambassador's residence. However, of equal if not greater importance for his future career was the extensive travel in northern Italy that he undertook on his return to the Academy. Accompanied by his friend Archie Burroughs, whom he encountered by chance in England, Shutze visited numerous villas and documented their trip with abundant photographs, which he mounted in his design albums. The architecture of northern Italy held a special appeal to Shutze, and many of the villas he studied on this trip would serve as an inspiration during his professional life. Venice had also been reopened to visitors following the war's end, and Shutze included this city in his tour.

In addition to enriching his knowledge of Renaissance and baroque details, the northern Italian villa provided an arrangement of building, garden, and site

38. *Howard Theatre,
Atlanta, Georgia,
1919–20
(demolished), principal
facade.*
39. *Theater interior.*
40. *Entry vestibule.*

that Shutze developed into a conceptual scheme for house siting in Atlanta. In diagrammatic terms, the northern villa consists of a casino (house) with designed gardens sited on the slope of a hill in the country but near a city. The architecturally significant facade of the casino faced a road or river that gave access to the house. Over time the original means of approach to the Italian villa often changed so that the grand entry became an inaccessible facade, which was opened to the public only infrequently on significant occasions. The daily entrance to the villa occurred elsewhere in the building, and often it had not been intended in the original design to serve this function. Access to many villas in the Italian Veneto occurred by water, and when overland connections superseded river traffic, the villa was approached from a direction other than that originally called for in the plan. This rearrangement of the design also took place in the American South, where river transportation provided far easier access to isolated plantations. Westover and Carter's Grove on the James River in Virginia, or Drayton Hall on the Ashley River outside Charleston illustrate this refocus of arrival points.

Some Italian villas vary this concept. For example, a casino might be approached on axis to a principal facade that was never meant to serve for a daily entrance. Shutze experienced such a villa when he visited the Villa Cuzzano near Verona. The original approach to the villa was marked at the roadside by a pair of gates and tall cypress trees through which passed an axial drive leading to the main facade of the yellow stucco villa. When Shutze saw it in 1919, the entrance was, as always, in the rear courtyard. The axial entry drive led to an elevated terrace planted with clipped box in symmetrical undulating curves that stretched the full length of the principal facade. Shutze used the concept of first viewing an inaccessible formal garden facade, and then circling the building to gain access from a courtyard, in the Calhoun, Inman, and Ben Smith houses in Atlanta.

Visiting villas for study was sometimes quite a time-consuming process for the fellows. During the war years, many architecturally significant northern Italian villas were not occupied and it was necessary to apply to the army for permission to visit them. Owners of those that were inhabited sometimes took days to reply and grant a visitation request, and then the fellows frequently were subjected to the glances of wary gardeners who found their activities suspicious. The police twice accosted William Hough, and once they arrested and jailed him as a spy for three days.[35] The photographing and measuring of buildings was not fully appreciated by the local residents, it seems.

38

39

40

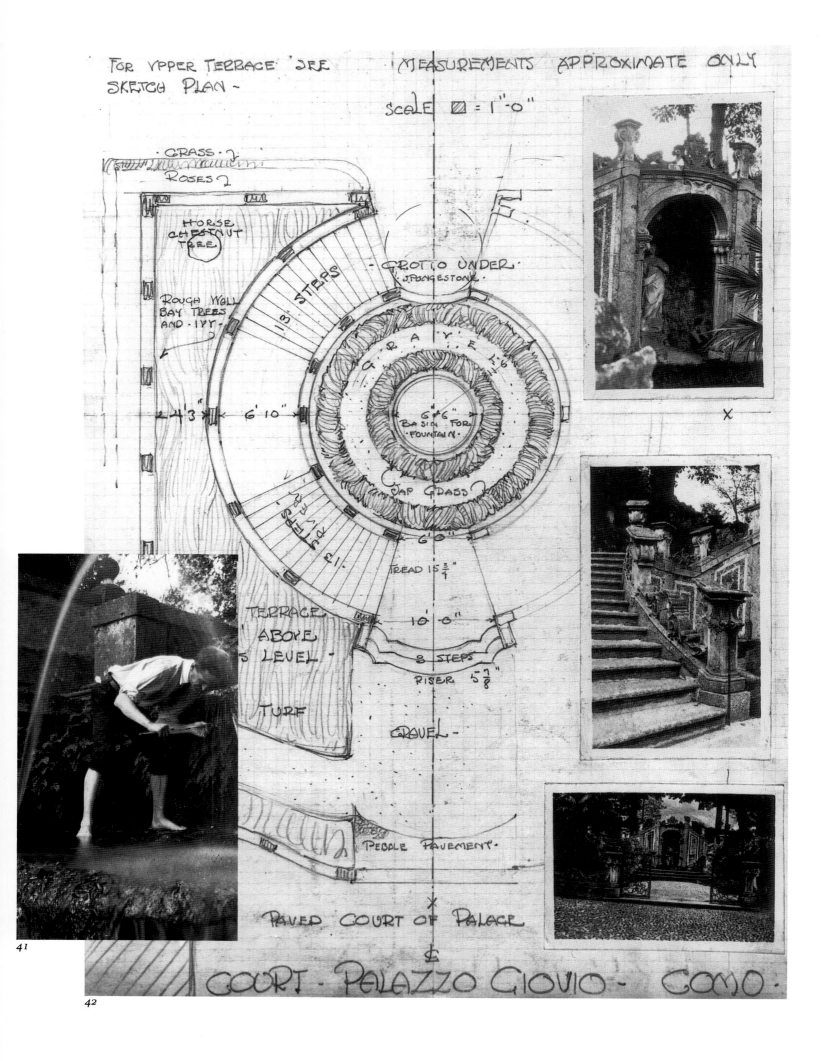

FOR VPPER TERRACE SEE
SKETCH PLAN -

MEASUREMENTS APPROXIMATE ONLY

SCALE ☐ = 1"-0"

GRASS ?
ROSES ?

HORSE CHESTNUT TREE

13 STEPS

GROTTO UNDER
SPONGE STONE

GRAVEL

ROUGH WALL BAY TREES AND IVY

4'3"   6'10"

6"6"
BASIN FOR FOUNTAIN

JAP GRASS ?

6'0"

TREAD 15 3/4"

TERRACE ABOVE
S LEVEL -

TURF

10'0"

8 STEPS

RISER 5 7/8"

GRAVEL -

PEBBLE PAVEMENT -

PAVED COURT OF PALACE

COURT - PALAZZO GIOVIO - COMO -

On other study travel, Shutze accompanied Edward Lawson, whose attention to plant materials and the details of the landscape surely nurtured Shutze's keen interest in his building settings (*figure 41*). Because the climate was so hot (as is Atlanta's), the palette of garden design in northern Italy is virtually limited to stonework, evergreen planting, and water. Color is achieved without flowers through the variety of green shades provided by box, yew, ilex, privet, grass, and lemon trees. The casino itself—with its stucco walls of colors such as yellow, tan, or pink—typically serves as the colorful accent in the garden. Fountains, pools, and cascades introduce coolness and sound into the Italian garden.[36] Whenever the opportunity presented itself, Shutze designed a landscape similar in many ways to those he had seen in Italy. In the hilly terrain of Atlanta, he typically placed buildings in elevated positions that visually dominated their sites, and he then surrounded the buildings with natural box or clipped box parterres to integrate the man-made geometry of the house with the wild nature of the untouched landscape. He often used a pink or yellow stucco building as an accent in the green landscape.

At the completion of his fellowship in 1920, Shutze returned to Atlanta to work for Hentz, Reid and Adler. Allyn Cox had been concerned that he might decide to do this, and in a letter to his mother during Shutze's final year at the Academy Cox wrote that,

> Shutze has just got back from America. He has been designing a most elaborate theatre, and doing a most awfully good piece of work. I think he hesitates between the sure-small work he would get in Atlanta, and the year or two he would probably have to wait before getting well started in New York. He is known in Atlanta, but it is a small place and he could never do so well there as in New York. You must help me to convince him, if he needs it, when you come over.[37]

For this perfectionist, his years in Rome refined his abilities and sharpened his concern for correct details into a nearly natural instinct. The Academy achieved its educational aims in Philip Shutze and had indeed provided a cultural basis for his career. Rome had taught him what to do, and Atlanta would now provide him with an astonishing array of opportunities to display his newly acquired knowledge.

41. Edward Lawson measuring the cascade of Villa Corsini, Rome.

42. A page from Shutze's Academy sketchbook, ca. 1919. His study of landscape details influenced his later professional practice.

The Atlanta
CITY BUILDER
OCT. 1931
Published by the Atlanta Chamber of Commerce

43. *Cover of The Atlanta City Builder*
showing Shutze's Citizens and Southern
National Bank in Atlanta, a renovation of
and addition to an earlier building.

II
THE CLASSICIST'S DESIGN
METHODOLOGY

44. Philip Shutze, ca. 1924.

In the decade following his graduation from the American Academy in Rome, Shutze established the design methodology that would serve him for the remainder of his career.[1] Shutze left no written explanations of his design methodology, consequently an understanding of his work must develop from an investigation of the buildings themselves. This study indicates that Shutze drew inspiration for new solutions to his clients' programs from what is termed documents in the French architectural tradition. Shutze's initial education at Georgia Tech and Columbia was an Americanized version of the Ecole des Beaux-Arts in Paris, and from these schools he was introduced to the study of documents as a method of developing a design. In Rome, this approach received further refinement with Shutze's introduction to on-site measuring of historic buildings. While at the Academy, Shutze employed three methods of producing study documents: the recording of building measurements, the creation of photograph albums, and the initiation of an architectural library. Each of these types of documents influenced his design production.

In Rome his experience "on the ladders" necessitated attention to detail, and the labors of these measuring expeditions resulted in four notebooks devoted entirely to recording information that had been obtained with great care and difficulty. He produced plans and elevations with all measurements meticulously noted; he entered in his books even the diameters of balusters and the individual moldings composing column bases or capitals. In addition to line drawings and black-and-white photographs, he recorded color palettes of mosaic floors as well as his observations on building colorations with descriptions of the raw sienna, burnt umber, or chamois ocher of the villas he visited. While a student, Shutze never noted how he intended to employ this arduously obtained information, but he subsequently found use for the measured details in projects like the Citizens and Southern National Bank in Atlanta, and he surely referred to his notes in selecting colors for his many stucco buildings.

In addition to his measurement notebooks, Shutze devoted enormous effort to the organization of purely photographic scrapbooks created from his own photographs and from purchased prints. His own photographs record the buildings and gardens he studied during his travels through Italy, and his thirty-four Italian scrapbooks organize the purchased photographs according to specific topics—doors, ceilings, fountains, sculpture, gardens—or building types, such as villas in

Rome or churches, to make the visual information easily accessible for later reference.[2] Shutze's purchased photographs came almost exclusively from Alinari, a specialized supply company that still provides large, professional close-up views of building details or buildings in elevation. The excellent quality of these photographs also made them ideal subjects for study. The Alinari scrapbooks cover both the well-known examples of Italian architecture and an equal number of buildings that would have been unfamiliar to an American architect. Although his scrapbooks encompass the historical styles from Roman to baroque, the majority of his images date to the mid-sixteenth through eighteenth centuries and affirm his interest in mannerist and baroque architecture.

Upon his return to America in 1920 Shutze continued to collect images, and he produced additional study scrapbooks topically arranged in a manner similar to the earlier Alinari collections. Later scrapbooks included images cut from magazines of English and American architecture and also numerous photographs of southern architecture taken during study tours. These books also included measured drawings published in architectural periodicals, but Shutze apparently never again found the time, or perhaps the need, to measure buildings himself. The total number of scrapbooks ultimately reached sixty-seven, and their condition indicates years of extensive use.

Shutze also relied heavily upon the library which he began to assemble while in Rome. Hentz and Reid introduced Shutze to the concept of an office library while he was a student at Georgia Tech working in their firm. The Hentz and Reid collection was relatively extensive; an inventory of office equipment conducted after Reid's death in 1926 listed 168 volumes.[3] Shutze had been instructed in the significance of reviewing documents while developing an architectural design, and he demonstrated this design approach in 1915, when he selected Columbia University specifically for its fine Avery Library as the site to develop his Rome Prize *esquisse*.[4] At Shutze's death his collection contained 1,756 items. This office library included current architectural literature as well as rare books such as a 1601 edition of Palladio's *I Quattro libri dell'architettura*; it focused on Italian, American, and English architecture and landscape architecture. Many volumes confirm through obvious signs of use that this was a working library and not merely the assemblage of a collector. (A list of Shutze's books on Italian and English architecture and landscape architecture is contained in Appendix I.)

An early example of Shutze's work, the now destroyed Howard Theatre (1919) in Atlanta, presents an especially clear albeit simple example of Shutze's design approach (*figures 38–40*). Shutze developed his design by first selecting a precedent to study: "For the Howard Theatre I chose my prototype in the Chierecati [sic] Palace Vicenza—Palladio is after all the Bible—It was a bit of facadism but I could not resist."[5] Documentation of the Howard Theatre shows clearly the reference to the Palladian original, but Shutze transformed the Palazzo Chiericati by adding seventeenth-century Italian baroque details to the sixteenth-century model (*figures 45–46*). The only surviving study of the theater's facade incorporates the central five bays of the Chiericati, modestly adapted through the addition and deletion of ornamental details. Shutze enlivened the subtle rhythm of the Chiericati with an opulent baroque cartouche that surmounted the facade's outer arched bays. In Shutze's design, the palazzo's reclining pediment figures descend to mark the central bay of the first floor. These two ornamental features, plus the somber character of the alternating pediments on the second floor, show Shutze inverting the character of Palladio's design by placing the emphasis of detail at street level. The gesturing figures that ornament the theater's roofline also recall Palladio. Here Shutze alters his model by superimposing his personal taste for the baroque to create a new classical variant. The baroque details appropriately foreshadowed the ornate baroque detailing found in the theater's interior. Shutze knew the Palazzo Chiericati from his travel in Vicenza as well as from Palladio's *Quattro libri*, which contains some illustrations of this palazzo, but just how he used these documents in the Howard Theatre design is not exactly clear.

The Citizens and Southern National Bank in Atlanta presents a more complex and more complete example of Shutze's classicist methodology. He considered this building his greatest design opportunity, and for it he employed a multiplicity of sources from second-century Roman to eighteenth-century American.

The commission to create a new headquarters for the Citizens and Southern National Bank came to the firm of Hentz, Adler and Shutze in 1929. This extensive project entailed the renovation and expansion of the existing Empire Building, and the creation of an impressive banking room appropriate to the client's desired image for their recently acquired designation as a national bank.

The Empire Building, at fourteen stories one of the tallest structures in

45

45. Howard Theatre,
initial design of 1919.

46. Palazzo
Chiericati, Vicenza,
photograph from
Shutze's office files.

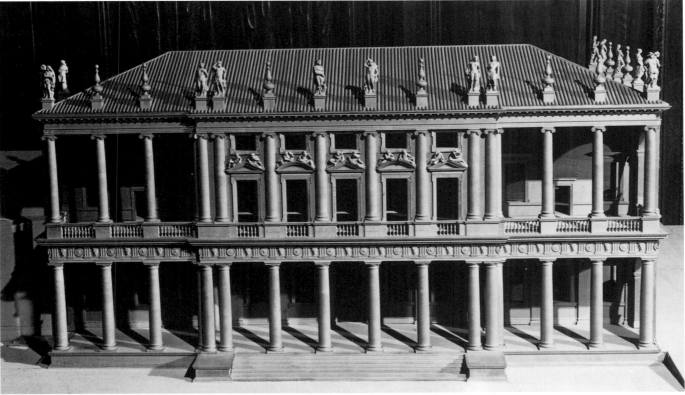

46

47. The Empire Building in Atlanta, of 1901, was renovated and expanded after 1929 as the Citizens and Southern National Bank.

Atlanta, had been completed in 1901 in the typical commercial style of high-rise office building developed in Chicago in the late nineteenth century (*figure 47*). At the sidewalk level, boldly projecting piers infilled with glass storefronts created an unexceptional utilitarian appearance. The original building, approximately 55-feet wide and 204-feet long, was constructed in the standard materials of its time, a steel frame encased in brick with terra-cotta trim. Shutze expanded the width of the building into the adjacent sites to bring the final size to approximately 80 feet by 204 feet. On the exterior, he stripped the first three floors of the older building of all their sheathing down to the structural steel frame, and he designed a new Renaissance inspired base to support the upper Chicago-style building (*figure 48*). Shutze considered the solidity of the new walls more appropriately symbolic for a bank than the commercial character evolved by the less substantial piers with their infill glass walls. To accentuate the new base further, Shutze retained the upper floors of the existing building and copied their design in the expanded office building.

With a new masonry sheathing of Indiana limestone, Shutze achieved the appearance of bearing wall construction, and he enhanced this illusion with deeply chamfered quoins at the building's corners and around the windows, with the continuous horizontal base along Broad Street, and with deep, blank niches inserted into the surface of the wall. The niches appear to have been developed to relieve the oppressive weight of the ponderous stone wall, but in fact they further the illusion of bearing wall construction by giving the appearance of great depth to the ornamental limestone wall, which is, in fact, only six inches deep. Shutze also used the detailing of arched openings around windows and the three banking room entries on Marietta, Broad, and Walton Streets to reinforce the illusion (*figure 49*).

In developing the new base, Shutze drew from his extensive knowledge of Italian architecture, and selected the work of Michele Sanmicheli (1484–1559) as the appropriate precedent for the study. The mannerist architect Sanmicheli created his most noteworthy buildings, particularly his city gates and fortifications, in Verona and Venice, and his vigorous designs symbolically answered the re-

40

48

50

49

48. Citizens and Southern National Bank, Atlanta, Broad Street facade.
49. On the Broad Street facade, Shutze created the illusion of masonry bearing wall construction.
50. Broad Street entry, detail of pilaster.

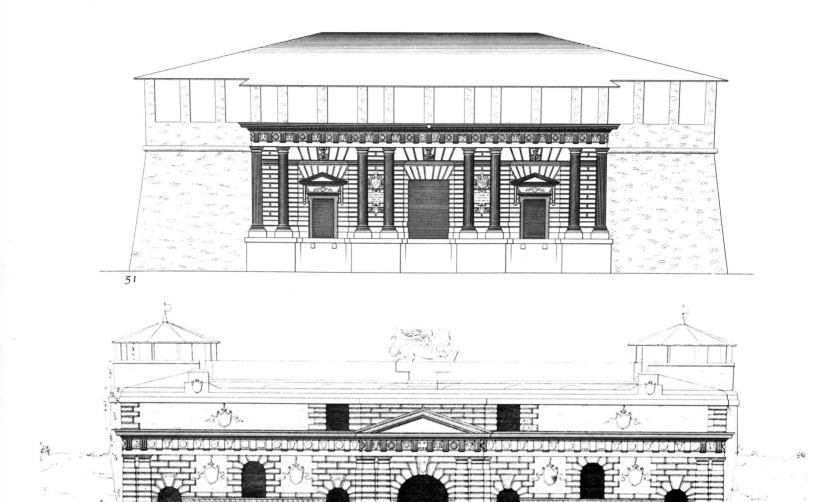

51

52

53

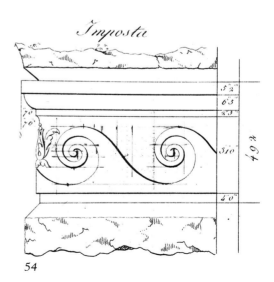

Imposta

54

51–54. *Illustrations from Zanotto's folio on Sanmicheli.*
51. *Porta Palio, Verona.*
52. *Porta Nuova, Verona.*
53. *Porta di Santo Zenone, Verona.*
54. *Porta Nuova, Verona, detail with a superimposed grid of pencil lines for proportional study.*

cently-organized bank's need for an appearance of permanence and impregnability. Shutze learned of Sanmicheli's architecture from his travels as an Academy student, from his scrapbooks, and from his office library. In addition to his Alinari photographs of Sanmicheli's work, Shutze owned an 1879 folio edition by Francesco Zanotto titled, *Le Fabbriche civili, ecclesiastiche e militari di Michele Sanmicheli* (The Civil, Ecclesiastical, and Military Work of Michele Sanmicheli), containing line drawings and details drawn to scale.[6]

One ornamental detail Shutze developed from the Sanmicheli folio is the wave pattern molding he used at the spring line of the arches along Broad Street. A molding of this type is illustrated in other books that Shutze owned (notably the Robert Gould Memorial depicted in *Monograph of the Work of McKim, Mead, and White, 1879–1915* [1915]). This molding also was used in several Florentine palazzi illustrated in Shutze's photograph scrapbooks, such as the Palazzo Pandolfini (*figure 55*). Nevertheless, evidence found in Shutze's library indicates that the wave pattern detail may be attributed with certainty to Sanmicheli, who employed it on two gates designed for the city of Verona in the early sixteenth century, the Porta Nuova and the Porta di Santo Zenona. On each of these buildings the wave reverses curvature at the center points of windows or doorways (*figures 52, 53*). Shutze studied these arrangements and produced similar reversals in his bank design, but here he did not want merely to use the wave pattern in a manner similar to Sanmicheli's; he wanted to recreate Sanmicheli's exact molding. To accomplish this accuracy, Shutze placed a grid of pencil lines over Sanmicheli's drawings in the folio to permit a proportional rendering (*figure 54*).

Another of Sanmicheli's buildings, the Palazzo Canossa in Verona, may have suggested to Shutze the concept for the decorative treatment of window and door surrounds on the bank. The Palazzo Canossa was illustrated in the Alinari scrapbooks and the Zanotto folio, and the bank design shares some of its features. In Sanmicheli's building, a stringcourse occurs at the springing line of the arched openings that, by its dark shadow line, further unified the design (*figures 58, 75*). Palazzo Canossa and Shutze's bank both share the strong central focus of triple

55. Palazzo Pandolfini, Florence, ca. 1917, being measured by students of the American Academy in Rome.

56

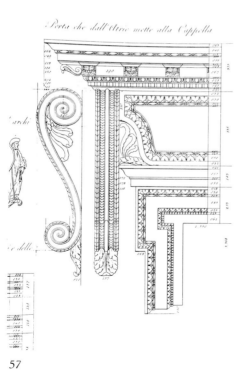

57

58

56. *Citizens and Southern National Bank, Broad Street entrance, showing flat-headed window (lower right) developed from a study of Sanmicheli.*

57. *Pellegrini Chapel at San Bernardino, Verona, detail with a superimposed grid of pencil lines for proportional study.*

58. *Palazzo Canossa, Verona, designed by Sanmicheli, in an Alinari photograph Shutze included in a scrapbook he compiled in Italy.*

59. *Citizens and Southern National Bank, detail of Broad Street entrance.*

arches, and the punched appearance of the second-story openings in the Palazzo Canossa correspond to the second- and third-story windows in the bank. Shutze designed the second-story windows as unrelieved holes in the masonry with no detailing, and these deep-set windows produced a dark black accent on the wall. Shutze made the third-story windows similar in size to the second, but treated them with rusticated quoins and voussoirs. With these details, Shutze tied the third-story windows strongly to the rusticated main level and directed attention away from the plain second-story windows. For purely functional reasons Shutze retained the second-story windows to provide light to second floor offices; the strong relationship between the third-level openings and the first level is set by Shutze's precedent. He uses the ornament to confirm the relationship, and, in this case, the precedent is a guiding inspiration, not an object that he imitated.

Shutze developed other details of the first-story windows, however, directly from designs by Sanmicheli. He treated all windows between the major arches and those below the wave-pattern string course with identical, flat ornamented heads (*figure 56*). This intriguing detail combined a scallop shell over swirling ribbons with a rectangular frame accented with acanthus leaves, and Shutze developed it from door heads of Sanmicheli's Porta Palio and the Pellegrini Chapel at Santa Bernardino in Verona. Although he did not repeat them at the same scale as the original, Shutze's details have similar proportions to the precedents. Both buildings are illustrated in Zanotto's folio, and Shutze's copy again shows signs of study with grids lined over the details (*figure 57*).

Shutze resolved the compositional problem of an uncentered entry, which he inherited from the original building, with an arrangement of overscale windows and doors. Across the length of the Broad Street facade are five major arches with four windows, one a blank. The remaining arch contains a side entry into the main banking room. This entry composition is the most elaborate detail of the facade and, apparently, Shutze designed it without studying a specific precedent (*figures 48, 56*). He took the true fourteen bays of the upper high-rise office floors and so arranged them on his remodeled level of the first three floors that he eliminated one bay to create a centered composition of thirteen bays. He used triple giant arches to strengthen this new compositional center, but the new focus is a blank window within a blank arch. This device endows the design with the mannerist attitude of knowledgeably rearranging classical elements—an attitude that always attracted Shutze.

The stacked ornamental elements of the arched entry also have a mannerist character. Inside the giant arch, with its rustication and overscaled console/keystone, is another rusticated arch capped with a pediment and backed with a thermal window (*figure 59*). The rusticated blocks of the inner arch do not correspond in size to those of the outer arch; they diverge from Sanmicheli's precedents, which always have running joint lines through the masonry work of superimposed arches. The differing sizes of rustication cause the inner arch to appear more deeply set and more delicately detailed.

The pediment is also distinctively mannerist. This element, which matches the other facade pediments in size and detailing, is interrupted by a block that protrudes through and above the tympanum surface to become the base for a globe surmounted by an eagle (reported by contemporary newspapers to be a stone copy of a bronze eagle in the Vatican). Shutze used the eagle as an ornament throughout the bank to evoke nationalism. He also used symbolic torches, composed of a block surmounted by a stone sphere, and a stone shield bearing the date of renovation. Working drawings for this entry show a male head as the

46

60. Citizens and Southern National Bank, elevator lobby adjacent to Broad Street entrance.

keystone decoration, rather than the shield; this head as keystone detail also appeared in Sanmicheli's Porta Nuova and Porta Palio in Verona, and Porta di Lido in Venice.

This mannerist entry composition leads into the elevator lobby; a plaster ceiling of Pompeian character decorates the surface of its intersecting vaults (*figure* 60). The entry to the main banking room occurs beneath a plaster eagle (*figures* 61, 62), whose wings are spread within a laurel wreath bedecked with ribbons. Shutze probably developed this motif from the Alinari photograph in his scrapbooks that depicts a bas relief in the Church of the Holy Apostles in Rome, earlier located in Trajan's Forum. This same detail was rendered by a French Academy student in Rome and reproduced in D'Espouy's *Fragments d'architecture antiques*, of which Shutze had two volumes in his office library. Passing beneath this eagle, one enters the banking room, which is the great showpiece of Shutze's renovation (*figures* 63, 64).

In developing an appropriate civic space for this room, Shutze returned to perhaps the most universally admired building in Western Europe—the Pantheon in Rome, 118–128 A. D. (*figure* 65). While a student at the Academy, Shutze studied the Pantheon in greater detail than even the buildings for which he produced restoration drawings (*figures* 66–69). He collaborated with William Hough and other students in measuring the building and in total recorded twenty

61. *Citizens and Southern National Bank, entry to main banking room from Broad Street vestibule.*
62. *Main banking room looking toward Broad Street vestibule; eagle above entry is one of many Shutze employed to symbolize nationalism.*

63. Citizens and Southern National Bank, main banking room looking toward Walton Street entrance. Shutze designed the chandeliers as well as the brass tables with their check-dispensing "temples."
64. Main banking room looking toward Marietta Street entrance.

pages of notes, measured drawings, and photographs relating to both the interior and exterior of the Pantheon.[7] He developed details of pilasters, columns, and floor and wall patterns directly from the precedent. Of greatest interest are the principal decorative elements in each building, the aediculae or diminutive temple arrangements in the original which house ventilation ducts in the banking room.

Shutze used the information he had assembled in Rome to achieve great precision in his detailing. A comparison of the column base in the bank with Shutze's measurements made at the Pantheon and recorded in his sketchbook shows that the banking room column base is almost an exact one-half scale reproduction of the Pantheon base. He reproduced the moldings identically, except for a one-quarter inch deviation in the lower torus molding and the upper fillet, and a one-sixteenth inch deviation in other moldings between these two. With such meticulous attention to detail Shutze endowed the entire design with a sense of correctness. Further comparisons of column heights and base diameters show that in the bank the base diameter to column height is proportionally one-quarter inch greater than at the Pantheon, and the bank columns are only two and five-sixteenth inches less than the proportional relationship in the Pantheon.

In a similarly exact manner Shutze developed the aediculae details in the bank; the bank aediculae reproduce exactly the proportions of the original, but

51

66

67

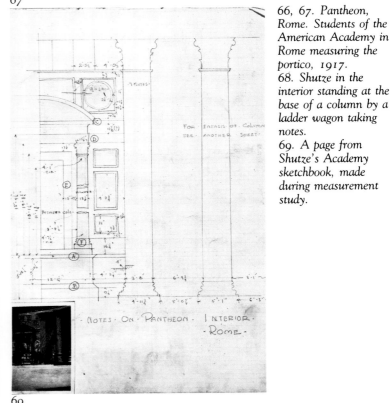

68

69

65. "The Interior of the Pantheon" by Giovanni Paolo Pannini, National Gallery of Art, Washington, Samuel H. Kress Collection (ca. 1740).

66, 67. Pantheon, Rome. Students of the American Academy in Rome measuring the portico, 1917.
68. Shutze in the interior standing at the base of a column by a ladder wagon taking notes.
69. A page from Shutze's Academy sketchbook, made during measurement study.

70

they are slightly larger than a one-half size reproduction of those in the Pantheon (*figure 70*). Shutze obviously used a proportional equation to develop these dimensions. Another decorative compositional detail that Shutze may have developed from his study of the Pantheon is his arrangement of two pedimented aediculae framing an arched opening. These larger compositional details are similar to the rhythm of pilaster-aedicula-pilaster arched openings found in the Pantheon.

Shutze also attended closely to other minute but significant details of the original. He used colored marble in the tympanum and frieze in his aediculae (*figure 72*). This unusual color treatment also occurs in the Pantheon aediculae, although the Pantheon employs a green marble and Shutze used ocher. And, in a manner similar to the Pantheon decoration, Shutze continued the colored frieze into the wall revetment as an accented band. This horizontal band functions in both the Pantheon and the bank as a subtle link between widely spaced major elements.

The materials Shutze employed in the Citizens & Southern National Bank produced a warmth that was lacking in the typical white classical detailing in the South. He created the warm honey interior tones by combining marbles from Georgia, Alabama, Tennessee, Utah, France, and Italy. This conception of brown-gold classicism also stems from the warm interior of the Pantheon.

Shutze developed this extraordinary banking space from his experience as an Academy student and from his detailed analysis of the Pantheon. But he did not simply reproduce details from the Pantheon; through his use of ornament and window elements, he transformed the circular temple precedent into a Renaissance passageway with second-story balcony windows opening into the banking space (*figure 73*). He enhanced the illusion of interior/exterior walls with an orthogonal layout that is the width of a typical street and makes a direct interior passage from Marietta Street to Walton Street. From any point within the banking room, street activity can be seen through glass entry doors. Shutze maintained the street illusion with arched openings that open the classically detailed somber and reserved banking space to a view of the intimately detailed and mahogany paneled officer's area, which is rendered in the American Georgian style (*figure 74*). A plate in Zanotto's Sanmicheli folio may have suggested to Shutze the balustraded arched openings that are so important to the street illusion (*figure*

70. Citizens and Southern National Bank, main banking room showing aediculae flanking the Broad Street entrance.

55

71

72

71. *Citizens and Southern National Bank,
wall detail in main banking room.*
72. *View of west wall toward officers' area
with second-story balconied windows above.*
73. *View from Marietta Street entrance
showing Shutze's use of exterior details to
create the image of a Renaissance
passageway within the bank.*

75). This elevation of the Palazzo Canossa in Verona shows a deceptively clear view of the hilly landscape far beyond. But Shutze did not take his balusters from the Palazzo Canossa, even though he had photographed and measured its balustrade and had entered the information in his scrapbook of redrawn details. He instead chose to study the details of balusters in the rear balcony of the Villa Lante, which he had also measured and recorded.

Shutze designed many interior furnishings to enhance the themes he had established in the architecture. For the main banking room he designed brass service tables in a Pompeiian style with delicately tapering footed legs supporting an eagle resting on a globe, and, to go with these tables, a brass temple that dispensed deposit slips.

The Citizens and Southern National Bank represents one design approach employed by Shutze in which his measured drawings from the Academy and from his office library provided specific details for a freely designed composition. He transformed the circular precedent of the Pantheon into a rectangular Renaissance street and he made Sanmicheli's city gates into details for a different building type. And, whereas Shutze probably developed the exterior arrangement from the Palazzo Canossa, the resulting design was far removed from the original model.

Those who admire classicism value a measured and continuous development of architectual design, instead of abrupt and discontinuous changes. The great challenge of the classicist designer is to extend his tradition by adapting it to new uses. The closer a design adheres to the model the greater the authenticity, but the less the creativity; the further the design deviates from the model, the greater the danger of unintelligibility or incoherence. By varying formal models and recombining formal elements, the classicist designer can create new images, but the problem faced is, how much variation can be tolerated before the model or tradition becomes incoherent? Shutze used his models in a variety of ways, and his best work adapts styles that self-consciously combined and juxtaposed classical elements. His interpretations of classical models are particularly subtle. These subtleties can be fully comprehended only by those who are familiar with the classical models, and it is especially difficult for those who are more accustomed to an ahistorical architecture dominated by abstraction and mathematical purity. Shutze's classicism demonstrates a flexible and versatile design method that offers an alternative in the ongoing search to reinvest humanist imagery in architecture.

74. *Citizens and Southern National Bank, looking from the officers' area into the main banking room.*

75. *Palazzo Canossa, elevation, from Zanotto's folio of Sanmicheli's designs.*

74

75

76. Calhoun House, Atlanta, garden facade.

III
SHUTZE'S CLASSICISM:
ITALIAN MODELS AND AMERICAN
APPLICATIONS

77. Philip Shutze at home, ca. 1935.

Shutze's professional career divides into two distinct phases that reflect the design opportunities provided through his varied professional partnerships. In his initial partnership with Hal Hentz and Rudolf Adler, Shutze established his reputation for creating finely detailed classical architecture. From 1923 to 1936, his clients included private individuals and small institutions—churches, universities, banks. With this clientele, Shutze freely exercised his own taste, and, after construction of the Inman house in 1928, he had firmly established his reputation as a designer.

Uncertain economic conditions notwithstanding, Shutze received numerous opportunities to develop a variety of historical styles. Prior to the depression, Shutze found clients who concurred with his desire to elevate domestic architecture by using the model of the Italian villa. In these suburban villas he made his most significant contribution to American architecture: this work explores the sensual nature of the Italian baroque, and the buildings both look and feel like the models they emulate. During the depression, he found few clients interested in flamboyant and exuberant architecture, and, for his palatial houses of the 1930s, he turned to the more reserved features of the English Regency.

I

From 1920 to 1926, Shutze worked in New York and Atlanta designing various projects.[1] In his attempts to establish himself in the unfamiliar and highly competitive world of New York, Shutze experienced frustrations he had never known in his native South. During the early 1920s, he worked for three separate firms in New York. With each firm, he designed proposals for projects that never materialized, and after several months with one firm he moved on to another only to face a similar fate.

Shutze had good reason to feel confident in his abilities when he decided to tackle New York. He had just completed one of the finest designs of his career—the Andrew Calhoun house in Atlanta (*figure 76*). The Calhoun commission originally came to the firm of Hentz, Reid and Adler in 1919. While Shutze was still in Rome, the firm produced a design that was vaguely Italian in character (*figures 78–80*). Although it featured Classical details and stucco walls, this initial

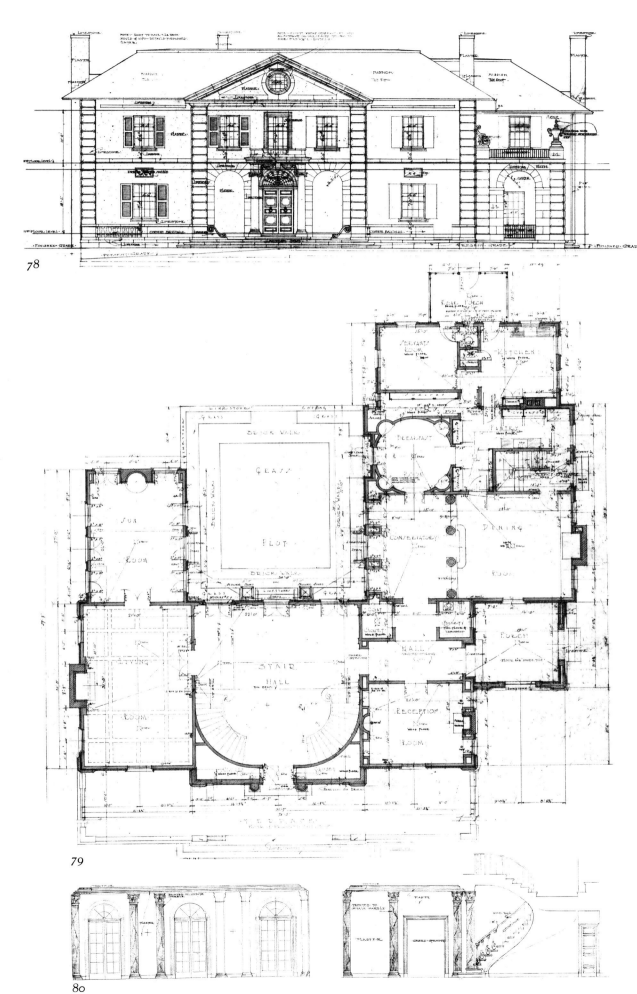

78

79

80

78. *Proposed Calhoun
House, 1919–20, not
designed by Shutze,
elevation.*
79. *Plan.*
80. *Section through
stairhall.*

design suffered from an overwhelming sense of untutored eclecticism. The projecting facade of the building was a symmetrical two-story mass with a centered entry, but the force of its symmetry was diminished by a two-story side wing connected by a one-story porch. Its interiors were even less thoughtfully detailed. One entered beneath a curving, double staircase which opened into a 30 feet by 30 feet one-story hall (*figure 79*). The enormous scale of this entry room dwarfed the living and dining rooms, which were approximately half its size. The original design called for formal interiors accented with marbleized columns and pilasters in transitional spaces and flat classical detailing within principal rooms (*figure 80*). This detailing also was uneven, with focal elements such as fireplaces unconnected to the surrounding plain walls. Fortunately, the clients abandoned their first site on Peachtree Street in favor of a more generous estate of over 100 acres on West Paces Ferry Road, an area then emerging as the new residential enclave of Atlanta society.

When the firm resumed the Calhoun project in 1922, Philip Shutze guided it into a spirited expression of the Italian baroque (*figure 82*).[2] Shutze later recalled that the family desired a house with an Italian character because they claimed a connection with the Farnese; the family name of Phinizy, it was said, derived from this connection.[3] The house reflected the northern Italian villas Shutze had visited on his return trip in 1919 to the American Academy, principally the Villa Cuzzano in Verona (*figure 81*) and the Palazzo Chiericati in Vicenza (which he had recently employed in the design of the Howard Theatre). The site plan arrangement of the Villa Cuzzano contained all the elements of the Italian villa models that Shutze used in planning his Atlanta residences. The Villa Cuzzano was approached through formal entry gates, and although these gates framed a view of the casino's formal garden facade, access to the house was through a rear courtyard. The gates, entry drive, and access point that Shutze devised for the Calhoun house all refer to this model: he placed the gates on axis with the theatrical garden facade to frame the public view of the house (*figure 83*); the entry drive first approaches the house, then circles to the rear courtyard where a quietly understated facade gives access to the house (*figures 84, 88*).

Shutze's design for the Calhoun house entry facade, drawn in 1922 and 1923, little resembles the original 1919 design. Similar in massing to the original, Shutze's version has a two-story mass, balanced on either side by subtly stepped

81

82

81. *Villa Allegri Arvedi, Cuzzano, near Verona, designed by Giovanni Battista Bianchi, ca. 1650, which Shutze visited in 1919 with Edward Lawson, and again in 1924.*

82. *Calhoun House, garden facade seen from the oval grass court.*

83. *Shutze designed the Calhoun gates based on his study of the formal entry gates to the Villa Cuzzano.*

83

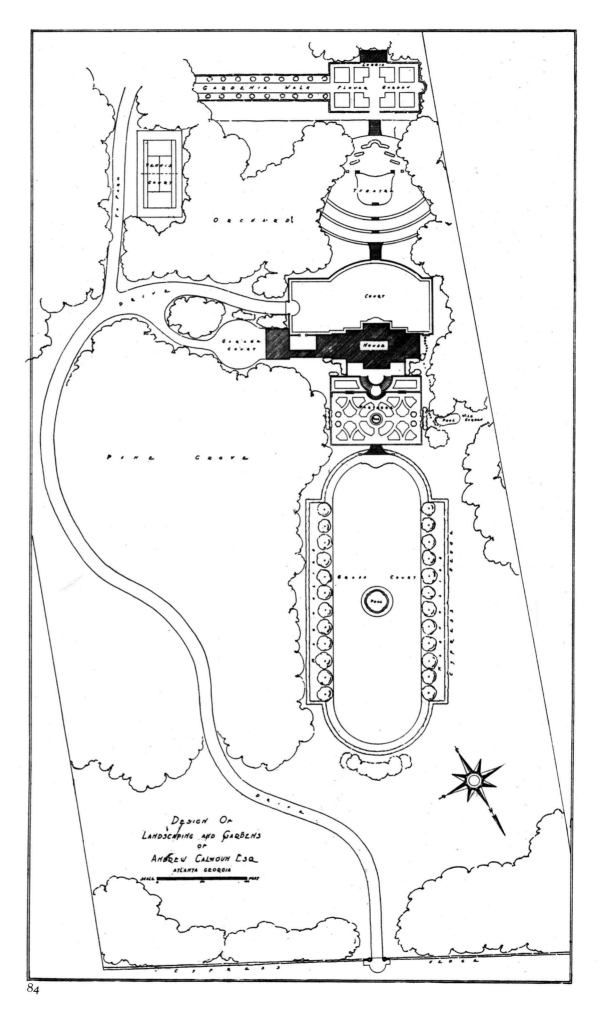

84. *Calhoun House, site plan. As in the Villa Cuzzano, access to the house is from the rear court; the gates, house, and gardens are on axis, following the Italian models.*

85. *Rear elevation taken from the working drawings prepared by Shutze.*

86. *Front elevation taken from the working drawings prepared by Shutze. The roof profile and triple-arched openings were developed from a study of the Villa Gori near Siena.*

REAR ELEVATION
Scale ⅜·1·0

HOUSE FOR
ANDREW CALHOUN ESQ
ATLANTA GA.

HENTZ, REID & ADLER
ARCHITECTS

7 | 396

85

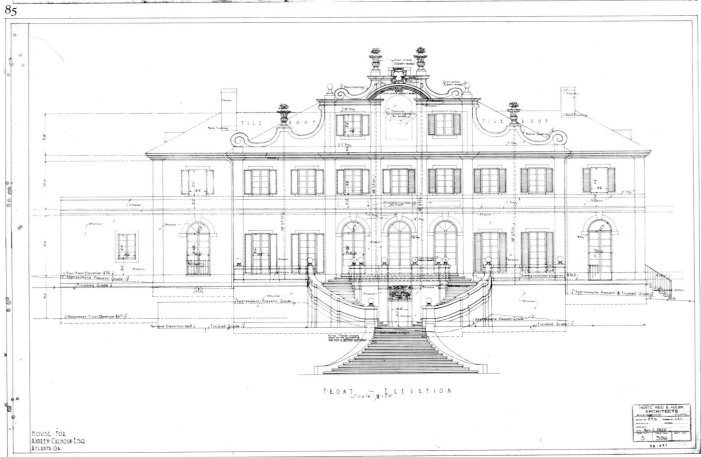

FRONT ELEVATION
Scale ⅜·1·0

HOUSE FOR
ANDREW CALHOUN ESQ
ATLANTA GA.

HENTZ, REID & ADLER
ARCHITECTS

5 | 396

86

87. Calhoun House, rear elevation. Shutze's color gradation of the stucco walls to create an appearance of age is evident in the central pediment and flanking walls.
88. Entry court.

89. Calhoun House, original parterre. The geometrically-arranged boxwood garden adjacent to the house follows the pattern established by the Italian villas that Shutze studied.

wings that produce a symmetry reminiscent of its Italian precedents (*figures 85, 87*). The original design employed mixed materials of limestone trim over what was mistakenly termed "plaster" walls. Shutze's design calls for stucco throughout, and walls detailed with projecting pilasters, arches, and keystones, as well as flat painted ornament. The 1919 facade is a textbook rendition of disparate Italianate elements; the second facade holds architectural details in dramatic tension just as its models do.

The exuberant baroque garden side of the house speaks eloquently of Shutze's revisions (*figures 76, 86*). This facade developed from a study of the Villa Gori near Siena, which Shutze visited as a student in the Academy; numerous photographs of this Tuscan villa appear in Shutze's scrapbooks (*figure 90*). The Calhoun house roof profile and central mass of the garden facade refer to similar elements at Villa Gori. Especially reminiscent of the precedent are the profile details of the segmental arch over pilasters surrounding a painted circle.

In plan, the design arranges intimately proportioned spaces into a coherent whole (*figure 93*). The main door opens into a small scaled, dimly lighted foyer and stair dominated by an Allyn Cox monotone sepia mural of a Roman historical

90. *Villa Gori, near Siena. The cornice profile, undetailed pilasters, and triple arches of the garden facade served as the inspiration for the Calhoun house.*

theme (*figure 94*). The cross axis of the hall connects to the dining room, drawing room, and library.

Many elements within the house are mannerist or baroque, and these contribute a personal expressive quality so characteristic of those styles. These elements further emphasize Shutze's break with the more sedate classical elements employed in the original Calhoun design: throughout the house Shutze contrasted two- and three-dimensional ornament to sensualize, so to speak, the space. A Borrominiesque surround complete with ears, frames the entries to the dining room and drawing room (*figure 94*). From the double French doors, which pocket into the wall, a short stairway leads down to the drawing room. Originally, the drawing room featured two Allyn Cox murals depicting Italian scenes. These have since been removed, but their painted frames remain as ghostly reminders of Shutze's original detailing. The mannerist character of the interior detailing is particularly evident in the contrasting details of the fireplace: rather than a typical composition of orders and moldings, Shutze used a simple molded surround that was surmounted by an expanse of fringed fabric hanging from swags and an active cartouche—all rendered in plaster (*figure 96*).

71

91. *Calhoun House. Double-curving stairs descend from the terrace to the level of the former boxwood garden.*
92. *Aediculae, surfaced with sponge-stone, ornament the wall enclosing the former boxwood garden.*

92

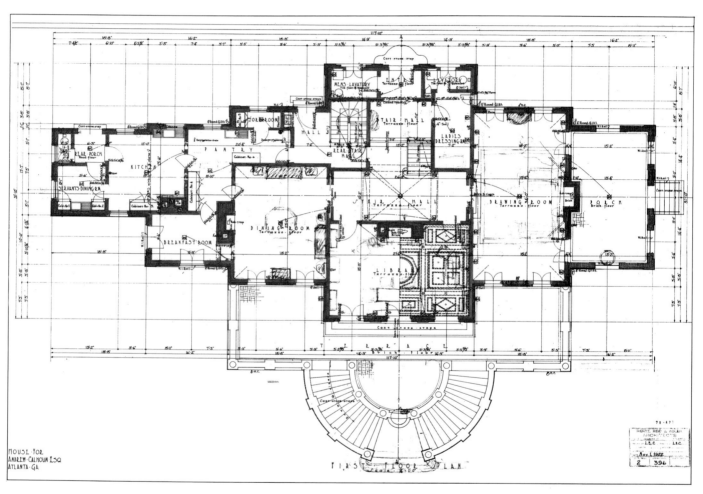

93. *Calhoun House. The first floor plan shows partial reflected ceiling plan from the working drawings; furniture has been sketched over the drawing.*

In the dining room, moldings on the fireplace front, door surrounds, and ceiling cornice are rendered in a bluish gray composition stone reminiscent of pietra serena, the stone accent typically used in Florentine villas and churches. A sculpted roundel of Michelangelo above the fireplace further strengthens this villa's Tuscan connections (*figure 95*). Shutze used thick stucco walls and terrazzo floors to realize a full range of sensory effects: these architectural elements sustain a feeling of cool dampness even during the South's hottest summers. The gesture is authentic: Italian designers used the same materials to combat unpleasant summer heat.

Shutze completed this Italianate villa by giving it centuries of age. Originally the exterior stucco walls ranged in color from deep burnt sienna at eave line to yellow umber at the base, and the trim was raw sienna. Shutze "aged" these exterior walls by applying dye to the wet stucco and then removing it with heavy sacking (*figure 87*). He graded the color as he had seen it in Italy, with the deepest tones in areas sheltered from the rain and the intense sun and with other areas left practically colorless as if the apparent exposure for centuries to the harsh elements had bleached the color from the walls.[4] The various effects Shutze created in this building are thoroughly convincing. The Calhoun house is as similar to Italian architecture as a classicist designer can produce.

In the second Calhoun plan Shutze also carefully adjusted ideal Renaissance proportions to actual spaces. In the principal rooms, he employed a proportional progression from 1:2 to 2:3 to 3:4. In the Renaissance, these relationships of room width to length were considered mathematically ideal, and therefore more likely to produce beautiful rooms.[5] Shutze would have learned of Renaissance proportions from many sources, including Palladio. In his Palazzo Chiericati in Vicenza, Palladio used three ideal mathematical proportions in sequence: 2:3, 3:3, 3:5 (12 feet by 18 feet, 18 feet by 18 feet, 18 feet by 30 feet). In the Renaissance, architect and client shared these intellectual concepts; in Shutze's time, these proportional interrelationships indicate the work of a finely educated designer.[6]

The Hentz, Reid and Adler office undertook many other important projects in the early 1920s, with Reid restricting himself to residential design and Shutze extending the features of the Italian villa to their apartment and commercial projects. For his elegant Robert Alston house (1922–23), Reid used Doric temples to balance each side of a Georgian central mass. By contrast, the Villa Apartments

94

94. Calhoun House. In the stair hall
between the living room and dining room, an
Allyn Cox mural faces the main entry.
95. In the dining room, seen here with
original furnishings, a plasterwork medallion
of Michelangelo, a Venetian-glass chandelier,
and a painted, footed table elaborate the
Italian character of the room.
96. In the living room, elaborate plaster
molding and Venetian chandeliers continue
the Italian character.
97. A view of the living room with original
furnishings shows a mural by Allyn Cox,
which has been subsequently removed.

95

96

97

project in Ansley Park (ca. 1920), exemplifies the authentic Italian character that Shutze brought to the firm's nonresidential work (*figure 102*). Here, Shutze achieved the appearance of an Italian villa through the ochre colored stucco walls and the floral swags and Tuscan columns applied to the planar entry wall. In a more formal spirit, the 696 Peachtree Apartments (ca. 1922) incorporate a typical Shutzean entry arrangement: a broken pediment above the entry door surrounding a second-story window, which in turn is surrounded by a swag of fruit and flowers (*figure 98*).

Shutze and Hentz jointly designed the Garrison Apartments (1923), now known as the Reid House; Shutze designed the facades, and Hentz the plans (*figure 101*). Height presented compositional problems to the classical designer whose design vocabulary more readily satisfied horizontal rather than vertical arrangements; through careful detailing, however, Shutze gracefully resolved this building's greater height. The mix of stone and brick, the subtle bow windows, and the imposing width of the entry facade help balance the vertical and horizontal dimensions. Especially refined is the detailing of the classical stone bucrania (bull's skulls) which adorn the cornice.

Rich's main department store is one of the firm's largest commercial buildings, and Shutze easily adapted the residential form of a Renaissance palazzo to a six-story palace of commerce (*figures 99, 100*). Founded by Morris Rich and his brothers in 1867, Rich's grew steadily until around 1920, when it experienced serious competition from the Chamberlin-Johnson-Dubose Company (located in a new five-story building built in 1918 in the Chicago commercial style) and the George Muse Clothing Company (located in a seven-story building built in 1921 with Renaissance details designed by Hentz, Reid and Adler). Morris Rich deemed the image of a new building important, and he purchased a corner site at Broad and Alabama Streets, which provided 421 feet of display windows. When the new building opened on 24 May 1924 with 180,000 square feet of floor space, it rivaled in size and amenities the largest mercantile stores south of Philadelphia.[7] Shutze detailed the building with an ornament that he developed from Borromini's Collegio di Propaganda Fide (ca. 1662) in Rome.

From 1923 to 1925 Shutze attempted, unsuccessfully, to establish his career in New York; little is known of this period. None of the major projects with which he was associated ever progressed beyond the design stage, and he met

98

98. At the 696
Peachtree Apartments,
the simple mass of the
building is enlivened
by a central stack of
classical details.

99. Rich's
Department Store.
The Renaissance
palazzo, adjusted to
accommodate glass
store windows at
ground level, became
a popular image for
American mercantile
establishments.
100. Detail above
entry doors.

99

100

101

101. *At the Garrison Apartments (Reid House), sheer massive brick walls are reduced in scale by the application of bow windows and stone detailing.*

102. *Color and ornament of the Villa Apartments evoke an architectural image of Rome.*

103. At the Massee Apartments, as with other large projects, Shutze demonstrated his ability to provide classical detailing for a vertically-proportioned building.

none of the success he had known in Atlanta. Columbia University offered him a teaching position, but he preferred to work with an architectural firm. Murray Hoffman, an acquaintance from Rome, invited him to work in the office he shared with his brother F. Burrall Hoffman, Jr., the architect of the Villa Vizcaya in Miami. In its day Vizcaya was perhaps America's finest example of the Italian baroque style. With the Hoffmans Shutze also spent several months working on the design of a large project titled "The Women's National Foundation," but funding for the project never materialized.

Shutze subsequently worked for the architect Mott Schmidt, who designed houses on Sutton Place for Mrs. William K. Vanderbilt II and for the theatrical agent Miss Elisabeth Marbury. For the latter project, Allyn Cox painted a hall with Chinese figures, and Shutze assisted with the menial labor by preparing the cartoons for pouncing. He also helped Frank Markoe with a charity street fair on Park Avenue. Shutze's design sketches and model were exhibited in a Best & Company display window. When asked later about his years in New York, he wrote that "[t]hese were not lost or wasted entirely—for one discovered what difference there was between 'going it' alone in a new and strange ambiente and a fine, well organized office among old friends and a first-rate clientele."[8]

Meanwhile in Atlanta, Neel Reid's health continued to decline, and Shutze was invited to return to Atlanta to become a partner in the firm of Hentz, Reid and Adler.[9] Without a designer, the firm was, as Shutze put it, "limping along," and it had accumulated a large backlog of projects developed in association with other firms. This number of supporting relationships did not occur again in the firm's history.[10]

In 1925 and 1926 Shutze extended to the firm's largest commissions—the Massee Apartments (in Macon) and the Atlanta Athletic Club—the Italian Renaissance, mannerist, and baroque models from which he had adapted his smaller buildings. Like the Garrison Apartments in Atlanta, the Massee Apartments indicate clearly Shutze's mastery of the design problem created when a classical style must be imposed upon a vertically proportioned building. Shutze elongated the Massee entry to give it the mannerist quality he had learned to

104

104. *Atlanta Athletic Club. For this eight-story building, now demolished, Shutze emphasized the horizontal rather than the vertical lines of the classical composition.*

105. *Elevation. The lower four floors contain the major public spaces and the upper four accommodate the guest rooms.*

106. *The building's functional variety is evidenced by the swimming pool and gymnasium in the central segment, and the public spaces, guest rooms, and roof terrace in the taller portion.*

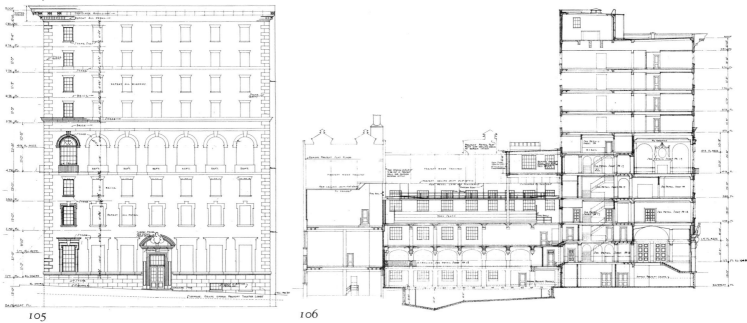

105

106

107. Rhodes house. The central portion of the design was inspired by the Scuola dei Tiraoro e Battiloro in Venice (figure 109). 108. Like its design precedent, the walls of the Rhodes house were originally tinted pink. The axial drive, originally intended to be accented with cypress trees such as those Shutze knew from Italy, was planted with pink dogwood after the cypress failed to thrive.

107

appreciate in Rome (*figure 103*). The base and overscaled pediment cartouche connect the design across the intervening floors and almost overcome the proportional difficulties created by height.

For the eight-story Atlanta Athletic Club Shutze addressed the height problem through careful attention to functional organization and visual expression; rather than accentuating height, he emphasized the horizontal lines of his classical composition (*figures 104–106*). The building's program included a complex array of athletic facilities, hotel rooms, and formal public spaces. To create a coherent expression that clearly acknowledged the building's diversity, Shutze produced a design of two equal units: the first four floors of public spaces formed a base for the next four floors of hotel rooms. The overall massing of these lower four floors approximated that of a Renaissance palazzo. Shutze extended the palazzo imagery with the four distinct levels of windows organized beneath what appeared to be a cornice, but was in fact two strips of stone surrounding a space of brick wall. The individual window designs represent the nature of the functions housed at each level. Shutze created twenty-one foot ceilings for the major public rooms on the first and fourth floors and he represented these significant spaces on the

facade of his building with grandly scaled twelve-foot high triple-hung windows. The stone quoins at the building's corners and its deep copper cornice further settled the design into a scale more reminiscent of the palazzo model than the modern high-rise.

Shutze carefully detailed the public rooms to create individually appropriate characters ranging from the delicate chinoiserie of the ladies' reception room to the somber intimacy of the wood-paneled men's lounging room and the elegant appointments of the Crystal Dining Room, so named for its chandeliers. (The men's lounging room became one of the local shrines for Bobby Jones's memorabilia including trophies, golf clubs, and his portrait on the green in front of East Lake Country Club.)[11] The public rooms also included fifty-one hotel rooms, and dining, meeting, and reception rooms, as well as a maze of athletic facilities: a twenty-five-yard swimming pool, indoor running track, handball courts, basketball court, weight room, and steam room. Although it was unequaled in Atlanta as an elegant multipurpose facility, the club was demolished in 1973.

During this same period prior to Shutze's attaining full partnership, Shutze and Reid probably collaborated in designing the Joseph D. Rhodes house on West Paces Ferry Road (*figures 107–108*). The style and the timing suggest collaboration: the design carries the strong impress of Shutze's interest in Italian architecture, and it was completed just before Reid died.[12] Relatives of the owner recall that Mrs. Joseph D. Rhodes "originally wanted a colonial-style house, but she saw a model of a Venetian villa on Reid's desk and 'she loved it.' "[13] Perhaps Mrs. Rhodes saw Shutze's thesis from the Academy and became infatuated with the Italian baroque; more probably she saw one of Shutze's photographs of a Venetian building, and he then used this image as the design precedent for her home. In any case, Shutze developed the entry facade, which is approached directly on axis along an avenue of pink dogwoods, from a detailed study of a small baroque building in Venice, the Scuola dei Tiraoro e Battiloro (1711), which he had photographed during his travels (*figure 109*). Shutze adapted its central stack of elements, and especially the overlapping curves and countercurves of the entry door surround, with only minor modifications. His greatest change was the addition of side wings and a porte cochere to expand the tiny Venetian facade from a vertical motif to a horizontal composition. Another significant aspect of the scuola was the bold color scheme of red with white trim. The red is a traditional

109. The Scuola dei Tiraoro e Battiloro of 1711 is located next to the baroque church Santa Stae on the Grand Canal in Venice; Shutze made numerous photographs of the small building and later employed it for the design of the Rhodes house.

Venetian color achieved from adding ground roof tiles to the stucco. Shutze and Reid intended to use the Venetian red, but the owner softened it to reddish pink, which Shutze graded as he did the exterior walls of the Calhoun house.

For five years, Neel Reid suffered from the brain tumor that claimed his life on 14 February 1926 at the age of forty-one. Both his personality and his strikingly handsome appearance remained in the public's consciousness long after his death. The persistent desire to credit Reid with work he had not designed, even commissions received by the office years after his death, must have irritated Shutze.[14] Although Reid had received an education comparable to that of most of his contemporaries, his training in no way matched the unusual preparation Shutze received for his career as an architect. In notes written late in his life, Shutze referred to Reid as a delightfully talented amateur; Reid was "sensitive and had a liking and a certain innate flair for all things beautiful and particularly for architecture."[15] Shutze appreciated the opportunities Reid offered him within the firm; as a memorial, he designed the simple funeral urn that marks Reid's grave.

II

After Reid's death Shutze assumed the uncontested position of designer within the firm, and according to later associates he designed everything the office produced.[16] By 1927, when the firm's name changed to Hentz, Adler and Shutze, the office's partners had developed an ideal balance of abilities and responsibilities. Hal Hentz, a highly respected and socially well-connected man, conducted most of the firm's business arrangements; Rudolph Adler handled construction and supervised the work; Shutze, as the design partner, ran the office as a strict hierarchy. Unlike many of his contemporaries, he did not continue the comraderie of the school atelier into his professional role, and he remained aloof from his draftsmen. The success Shutze enjoyed in his career resulted in large measure from the perfection of his partnership. His personality was not entirely suited for filling all dimensions of an architectural practice, and his first partners allowed him the freedom to design while they handled other essential matters.

Shutze had an especially acidic personality, but his friends and clients considered his conversation clever and entertaining. Virginia Campbell Courts, a friend for over forty years, recalled that "his lines were so witty, somewhat reminiscent of a Noel Coward play."[17] She felt that plain statements would have bored Shutze and that he enjoyed his caustic opinions: one might be annoyed at his comments, but never bored. Like Mrs. Courts, other acquaintances always recalled his careful enunciation, to which he gave further emphasis with his voice and enormous attention to the timing of his words.

In his professional life, Shutze spared himself from polite restraint, preferring to set hair on end with his barbed remarks. His self-assurance in matters of design and the recognition he received from others encouraged him to run his office autocratically. For each project, Shutze produced detailed and accurately proportioned sketches within his private office; these his associate James Means drafted for him.[18] Then began a meticulous process of study and refinement with Means producing many studies for Shutze's criticism. Shutze seldom engaged in the drafting of working drawings, but his initials are found on sheets of details that required his special drafting skills. He also produced the office's renderings, yet for these he never employed the laboriously rendered Beaux-Arts drawing techniques he had used with such finesse during his student years. As a practicing

architect, he found those magnificent renderings to be a waste of effort, time, and money. For office purposes and for presentations to clients, he developed a technique using colored pencil on tracing paper. He rendered elevations, the preferred view in the Beaux-Arts system, rather than perspectives, although he drew perspectives with great facility and used them for his own design studies.

Shutze invested the backlog of projects that had developed from the period of Reid's illness with his own preferences for Italian architecture. The East Lake Country Club, which Shutze had helped design in 1914 in an early English Renaissance style (*figure 8*), was severely damaged by fire in 1926. Although nothing of the exterior called for a classical interior, Shutze nevertheless reworked the club's paneled walls and ponderous interior detailing in lighter and more formal classical details (*figure 110*). These new interiors connected the town club stylistically with its country club even though the Atlanta Athletic Club was thoroughly classical and the brick and stucco exterior of the East Lake Club was restored to the style of an English manor house.

The Edward Inman house (*figure 112*) was the firm's most important project during the 1920s; it is surely the one that has proved to be the most lasting memorial to Shutze's diverse abilities. Both client and designer lavished great attention on the design, and they produced a remarkably graceful statement of style and taste. Like the Calhoun house, the Inman house offered to Shutze the opportunity to use all the aspects of his training: from site planning and garden design to the creation of a new architectural order.

111. The Inman House is also known as the Swan House, and is the home of the Atlanta Historical Society. Site plan, drawn by Clay Ulmer.

The house is sited within a hilly, lush green landscape, typical of Atlanta's Piedmont location, and within the north Atlanta residential area of Buckhead. The extensive estate borders two major streets and offered numerous satisfactory building sites. Shutze placed the house adjacent to the site's high point above Andrews Drive to give it a commanding view of the landscape, which dropped away in three directions (*figure 111*).

In Mrs. Inman, Shutze found a sympathetic client who shared his love for architecture. At her request, he studied the work of William Kent, and he adapted for his time Kent's early eighteenth-century English adaptation of Palladio. Shutze's design is a lesson in the integration of classical forms.

The project began in 1926 with an elaborate design that proved too costly. The built design retains Shutze's original concept, with adjustments occurring principally in massing: second floor rooms were deleted from each side of the original composition, and the central projecting facade was also reduced. The original central facade displayed statues of the four seasons in a Palladian fashion at the eave line, but the realized project retained only Summer and Autumn (*figures 113, 114*).

Except for very brief remarks, Shutze never wrote about his architecture, but he prepared a rare description of the Inman house, or Swan house as it was named, which illuminates his design approach and the architectural elements upon which he placed greatest value:

There was no attempt to adhere slavishly to any predetermined style or period for the design of the Inman House as to exterior, interior, furnishing and landscaping. Generally speaking the house may be placed in the first quarter, or better, the first half of the 18th century. It was the owner's desire that this be done. . . .

As Inigo Jones had dominated the first half of the 17th century and Sir Christopher Wren the last half—so had the Earl of Burlington created the full Italianate School in the first half of the 18th Century—along with the

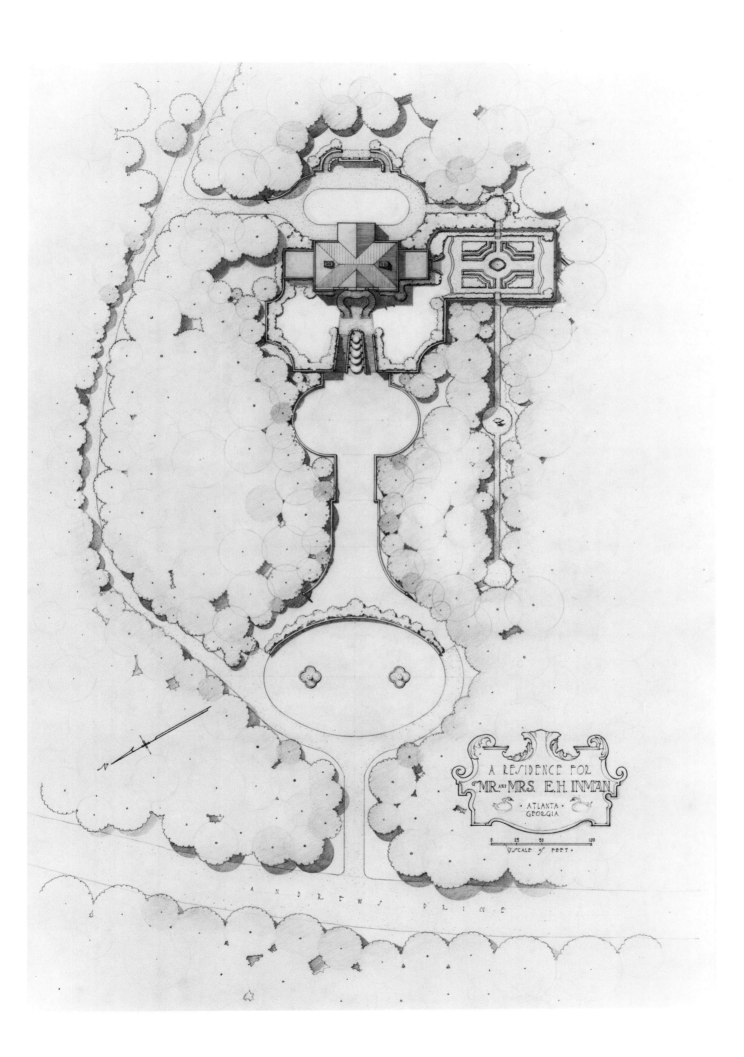

A RESIDENCE FOR
MR AND MRS. E.H. INMAN
· ATLANTA ·
GEORGIA

0   25   50   100
SCALE OF FEET

112. At the Inman house, the slope of the land is shaped by terraces and walls, and accented vertically by fountains, obelisks, and urns; the fountain cascade forms a compositional base for the garden facade.

113

114

group that formed around him Leoni, Colin Campbell, William Kent etc.—
Lord Burlington had travelled extensively in Italy—studying Palladio, collecting works of art arriving back in England and coming of age in 1716.

There is no prototype existing in England that served as a model for the present house as a whole. As to details many have been adapted. The first draft of a house, which, incidentally, proved too costly was inspired by Bramham Park in Yorkshire entirely Queen Anne in Period, (Queen Anne died in 1714) yet a fine example of the Italianate School with characteristically extensive gardens in the grand manner.

113. Inman House, garden facade, drawn by Shutze.
114. Entrance facade, drawn by Shutze.

In our existing house the only remnant of Bramham is the horse-shoe stair. No doubt this feature came to Bramham by way of Fontainebleau.

The name Swan House was entirely of Mrs. Inman's choosing and could not have been derived from an English example. It is true that there are smaller houses such as the small house of the Wren Period in Chichester of that name taking its title, no doubt, from two curious birds a-top the gateposts and resembling ostriches or even emus rather (emus were probably unknown in Wren's time) there is another 19th Century House in Chelsea of that name.

It is more likely that Mrs. Inman was more influenced by such things as the regal splendour of the Swan as belonging to the Queen.[19]

These passages indicate that Shutze's knowledge of architecture was not restricted to the mere appearance of historical details, but included an academic concern for and understanding of how in the seventeenth and eighteenth centuries the English adapted the sixteenth-century Italian villa for a new use in a new climate with new materials.

Shutze continued his detailed description beginning with the exterior arrangements (*figures 115–117*):

The existing main entrance to the grounds from Andrews Drive is by way of an earth bridge (culvert) and leads directly onto a broad expanse of turf where two large water basins are located—the road appears to divide here. The right undeveloped. The left branch—sweeping past the retaining wall with its ivied recessed arches and holding rising terraces up to a cascade on the axis of the Horse-Shoe Stair—climbing up the sloping hill and finally arriving at an enclosed court partly paved with cobble stones. A very char-

115

*115. Inman House,
entrance facade and
arrival court.
116. Detail of Roman
Doric portico and wall
ornament.
117. Portico.*

116

acteristic feature. Against the hill, a retaining wall with niches and flanking stairs that mount to a higher level is situated opposite the large Doric portico which shelters the drive to the entrance door to the house and this is flanked by niches with decorative urns.[20]

In describing the interiors, Shutze expressed his awareness of precedent, and his usual concern for interior details (*figures 118–129*). Beginning with the main entry beneath the Doric portico, Shutze wrote:

> The visitor enters a round open-end hall with an ionic order, a black and white marble floor of roman design and is in fact a part of a more spacious oblong hall which contains the splendid circular staircase with bronze balustrade and walnut treads, fine carved doors and overdoors and ornamental plaster. Consoles, paintings, screens are noteworthy.
>
> From the great hall, at the left, through an archway is the library, a stately room with warm Wren-like panelling, with trims, cornices, overdoors, and archivolts carved to accord with the Grinling Gibbons style of decorations of the mantel and over mantel which were taken from a former house of the owners—the rug is a splendid foil as are the curtains.
>
> Across the hall is the grand dining room with its Queen Anne moulded ceiling its Waterford chandelier. Its Kent-like Aubusson rug and walnut floors. This room boasts the very important Swan Consoles Chippendale in period—The eagle sconces of such fine scale. The steel fireplace fittings, the Chinese wallpaper and the window cornices with their over-draperies and curtains—this room is finest in the afternoon or by candlelight. . . .
>
> And finally to the elegant morning room pale blue-green with curtains of the same colour but lower in key—engaged Corinthian columns on pedestals with capitals adorned with diminutive swans enclose the chimney breast of fine marble and Chinese pediment above—Sienna marble is used in surround and hearth—a most interesting feature is the window trim carved with gadrooning and resting on the chair-rail of dado and ending in a scroll.[21]

Shutze's description of architectural details conveys the richness of the room, but not the quality of the elements, especially the exceptional delicacy of his swan's head capital, which he designed for the morning room (*figure 128*). For his new classical order, Shutze employed the fluted shaft and general outlines of the Corinthian, but he substituted for the acanthus the gracefully curving neck of a swan emerging from twin lilies.

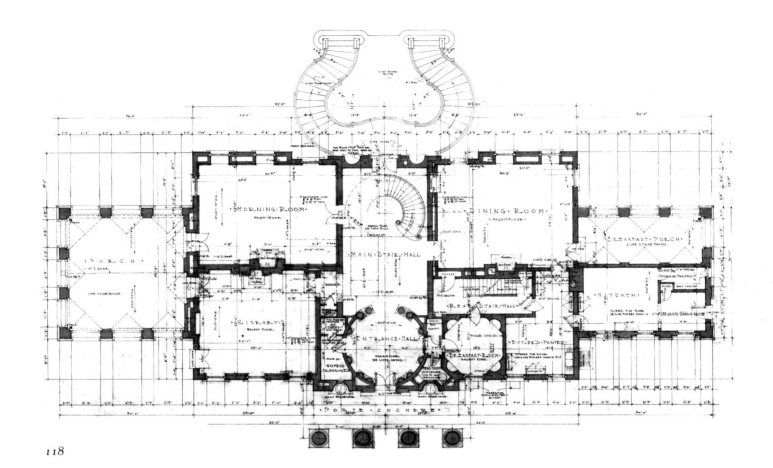

118

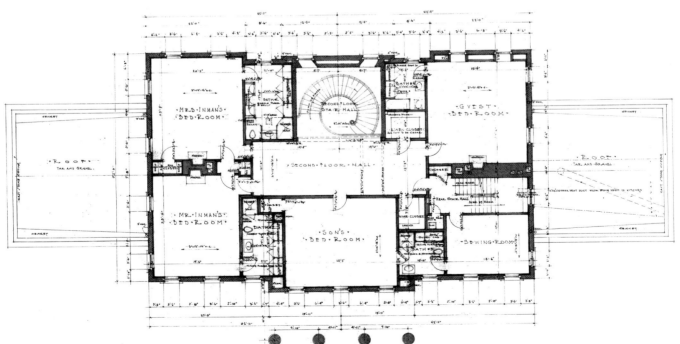

119

121

122

123

120. Inman House, circular entrance hall
opening into main stair hall.
121. Main stair hall looking toward library
and morning room.
122. Second-floor hall looking toward garden
facade.
123. Entrance hall, Shutze's study sketch.

124

125

124. *Inman House, dining room, study sketch by Shutze; the inclusion of furniture, paintings, lighting fixtures, and decorative porcelain typifies the architect's study sketches.*
125. *Dining room, study sketch by Shutze.*
126. *In the dining room, a Queen Anne molded ceiling is over the Kent-style Aubusson rug.*

127. Inman House, morning room. Engaged
Corinthian columns on pedestals flank the
fireplace; its surround and hearth are of
Siena marble.
128. Detail of column in morning room,
drafted by James Means. Shutze designed the
capital with lilies and swan's head in place of
the normal acanthus in the Corinthian order.

128

129. Inman House, library. The natural-
finished woodwork in this room contrasts
with the more delicate character of the other
rooms in the house.

106

The landscape design of the Inman house matched the thoughtful detailing of the interiors. Shutze employed two formal boxwood gardens at either end of the house to hide the transition from the Italian baroque garden facade to the startlingly different William Kent entry facade. The more important of the gardens opened off the library and morning room, and terminated with an arrangement of twin columns supporting broken pediments that surrounded a rampant eagle (*figures 131, 132*). To design these details, Shutze studied the garden ornaments in La Pietra, Il Pelligrino, near Florence. In the Florentine garden, the twin columns occur at ground level and are flanked by human figures. Drawings indicate that Shutze considered this arrangement, but substituted urns and the rampant eagle for the statues.

The water cascade beneath the baroque garden facade also employed an Italian precedent, in this case, the cascade at the Villa Corsini on the Janiculum in Rome (*figures 136, 137*), a building that Shutze knew well from his American Academy days. Shutze's scrapbooks contain photographs of Edward Lawson measuring details of the fountain. The cascade is merely one element in the Corsini gardens, but Shutze transformed it into the compositional base of Swan house to add movement and sound to his design. The cascade and its enclosing walls diminish inward toward the house; this forced perspective device increases the apparent length of the stairs and the cascade and aggrandizes their function as the base of the house.

To reflect the dual stylistic nature of the house, Shutze composed a landscape conceived from Italian themes and filtered through English experience. Referring to this design, Shutze wrote that "as to the landscaping whatever has been done was with the Italian garden in England in mind. Before the advent of Capability Brown, as in the Italian vernacular, there are no perennial flower borders as such; an architectural frame work with evergreen planting is the order—flowers are used in pots and tubs, a usage so common to the European arrangement in parterres with lemon trees as accents."[22] Because delicate flowers wither without constant care in hot summers, Italian gardens, like southern gardens, are green; azaleas, box, and camellias provide different shades of green and, in spring, vibrant masses of color.

Shutze proposed a landscape composition to accent the high point of the site, which rose above the oval entry court, but Edward Inman's sudden death

131

132

133

130. Inman House, boxwood garden
adjacent to library and morning room, seen
here upon entry from the oval arrival court.
131. Architectural elements accent the
enclosing garden wall; the twin columns with
broken pediments were developed from
ornaments in the garden of La Pietra, Il
Pelligrino, near Florence.
132. Detail of the garden ornament.
133. View toward the oval arrival court.

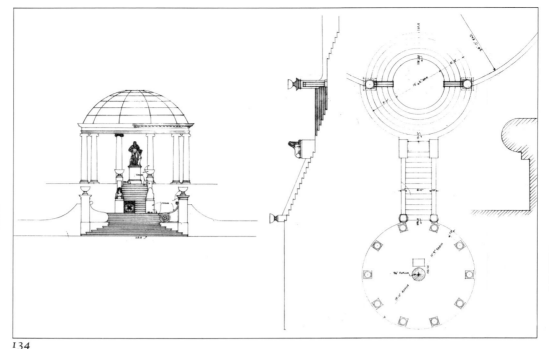

134. Inman House, proposed garden stair and temple (unbuilt). The stair was designed to rise from the arrival court to the ten-columned temple at the crest of the site. 135. The roof of the garden facade is accented with statues of summer and autumn.

on 15 April 1931 prevented its realization (*figure 134*). Shutze's design incorporated a stairway leading on axis from the Doric portico to a thirty-six inch diameter poplar tree at the crest of the site. He surrounded this magnificent tree with a ten-columned circular temple with an openwork domed roof acting as a wisteria trellis. In this temple, Shutze centered a classical male nude figure with a hunting dog, and leading up to the temple, he placed sphinxes to guard either side of the stair. This marvelous folly, evoking the image of a temple of love, was never constructed. Shutze's drawings date from December 1930, and at Mr. Inman's death such a garden folly became inappropriate. Instead, Shutze completed this area with a more formal and subdued arrangement of double stairs leading up to a landing with a simple water basin. He treated the wall facing the Doric portico with triple arches accented with sponge stone to simulate a garden grotto.

Shutze's two most complete residential creations—the Inman and Calhoun houses—demonstrate the variety he achieved with the model of the Italian villa. Both houses share the concept of an ornate baroque facade accessible to public view, but inaccessible by a direct approach. In each case one enters the private estate, views the house axially across carefully orchestrated gardens; then the approach veers off into a forest canopy to re-emerge in an oval courtyard facing a more restrained architectural facade. Although the two houses are conceptually related, their architectural characters differ completely: the Calhoun house is Italian, the Inman house English Palladian. The Calhoun house is intimately scaled and informal in plan, with few elaborate details; the Inman house has a

136

137

138

139

136. *Inman House, garden facade with fountain cascade. The walls of the stair converge slightly toward the house to emphasize the perspective of the fountain.*

137. *Villa Corsini, Rome, fountain cascade. Shutze and Edward Lawson studied this fountain in detail during their years in Rome; it served as the model for the cascade at Inman house.*

138. *Inman House, detail of the terrace and upper cascade.*
139. *Detail of the cascade and stair.*

140

141

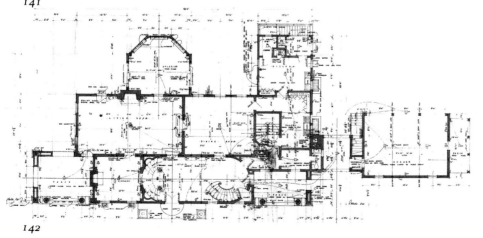

142

143

formal layout of a grand entry hall with public rooms opening from it and architectural details of an equally formal character such as classical orders with their appropriate detailing. Shutze designed the Calhoun house immediately after his student years in Italy, and more than any of his later architecture, it epitomizes the replication of that experience in solid architectural form. Created some years later, the Inman house provided Shutze the opportunity to synthesize Italian and English architecture and to explore fully the palatial scale of residential architecture.

Shutze's most important contribution to American architecture is his development of the Italian baroque tradition. A number of commissions in the 1920s and 1930s provided him with additional opportunities to extend and adapt his Italian forms, and several unrealized schemes indicate his virtuosity in the use of this historical style.

In the late 1920s the Childs and Horgan commissions offered him two such opportunities. The houses differ enormously in materials, scale, and appearance, but Shutze developed both of them from precedents in northern Italy. The Childs-Jones house (*figure 140*) is a mansion of major proportions sitting on a gentle rise not far from the earlier pink Venetian baroque Rhodes house. For the composition and exterior details of the Childs-Jones house, Shutze used the Barchessa Valmarano on the Brenta Canal, a building included in his Academy photograph albums (*figure 141*). Like its precedent, Shutze's design has the unusual feature of two double porches at each end of the main mass of the house. The centered entrance is accented with a roofline pediment and scrollwork above the entry door. In the Childs-Jones design, Shutze evoked an American version of the Italian precedent by simulating its stucco walls with painted wood. The columns and matched board siding, like those at George Washington's Mount Vernon, are finished with a sand enriched paint. The wood columns do not have a typical tapering profile, but are treated like stacked stone drums to elaborate further the designer's clever imitation of masonry architecture.

The Childs-Jones interiors are spatially intriguing with numerous changes in floor elevations (*figures 142, 143*). Entrance to the house occurs between the spiral stairs to the second level and twin stairs curving down to the library. Only the dining room is at the entry level and from it, or the entry hall, steps lead down to the living room. Shutze often orchestrated such spatial effects in his

140. Childs-Jones House, elevation taken from the working drawings, showing painted wood siding rather than the usual stucco.

141. Barchessa Valmarano, Brenta Canal, Veneto, photo from Shutze's Academy albums. Although details are similar, the size of the Childs-Jones house is greater than this precedent.

142. Childs-Jones House, plan taken from working drawings.
143. Shutze's study sketch of the stair hall.

144. Horgan House. The dramatic coloration of this house differs from the ochre tones of the chapel of Villa Cuzzano (figure 147), the precedent Shutze studied for this design.

145. Elevation.

146. Shutze reinterpreted the ornament of the precedent, but maintained the compositional arrangement of the original. Here, he substituted the vertical accent of a statue of the Virgin Mary and Child with a raised obelisk.

145

146

147. Chapel of the Villa Allegri Arvedi, Cuzzano, near Verona, which Shutze used as a precedent for the Horgan house (figures 144–146), and which he and Edward Lawson photographed in 1919.

residential designs, but never with greater effect than in the Childs-Jones house.

The Dan Horgan house in Macon (*figure 144*) shares only its development from Italian baroque architecture with the larger and more grand Childs-Jones house. Shutze created this delicate jewel from a study of the chapel of the Villa Cuzzano near Verona, a spirited baroque design approached from the courtyard below by way of a double staircase. Built in commemoration of a visit to the villa by San Carlo Borromeo, the chapel's composition appealed to Shutze, and he included numerous photographs of it in his albums (*figure 147*). The house and its precedent share the same active roofline and composition of two bay arcades surrounding a central mass. For this residence Shutze deleted ecclesiastical references and developed an ornamental system of floral swags and flower-filled baskets to celebrate the owner's occupation as a florist (*figure 146*). The house is colored a bold reddish-pink in the tradition of northern Italian villas. Shutze sited the house on the axis of the academic quadrangle of Wesleyan College, whose campus is located immediately in front of the house. In 1928, Shutze terminated this axis with his own design for the Wesleyan Library, a reserved English Regency design with a raised Ionic portico in marble.

The Morris Michael house in Macon was probably Shutze's last Italian baroque residence to be constructed (*figure 149*). Its facade shows much greater restraint in detailing than his earlier Italian designs. The commission was received contemporaneously with the May Goodrum house in Atlanta (*figure 186*), which in comparison with his earlier baroque designs is a reserved composition in the English Regency style. Michael asked for both Spanish and Italian features, and this direction as well as Shutze's growing interest in the English Regency may explain the greater simplicity of detailing. Nevertheless, the design is Italian in spirit with stucco walls, marble and terrazzo floors, and intimate walled gardens connected to the house with breezeways. In the living room, Athos Menaboni painted pilasters on the walls and marbleized wainscoting. In the library, the clients' desire for Spanish features was realized with a painted wood joist ceiling, twin columns supporting a beam, and a small fountain. The dining room was wrapped with a wall painting on canvas of Venice in winter, which Menaboni adjusted to fit the room's dimensions. Other elements such as the entry foyer and circular stair hall have English Regency details, and these give the impression that Shutze's thoughts were in transition.

In two unrealized schemes of the mid-1930s Shutze also employed the Italian baroque. Shutze's first scheme in 1936 for the Ben Smith house in a baroque style was rejected by the clients. The only surviving remnants of this initial scheme are the sweeping stucco entry gates, each topped with a large stone pinecone. In 1938 Thomas K. Glenn commissioned Shutze to design a house in Sea Island, Georgia, the favorite summer retreat of wealthy Georgians. Shutze returned to his Italian baroque models and created an exhilarating blend of undulating forms with appropriately nautical detailing (*figure 150*). The opulent character of the design probably reflected Mrs. Glenn's desire to create a notable house in Georgia's exclusive island resort.[23]

A rendering of the proposed main facade shows a rigidly symmetrical arrangement of projecting masses with second-story open porches capped by hipped tile roofs that surround an inner court and the entrance to the principal rooms. The design projects a delightfully appropriate image for a seaside summer retreat with its central focus of an undulating parapet wall, which crescendos in a triton and dolphin sculpture.

Shutze's interior sketches present a highly formal arrangement more like the

148

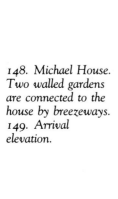

148. *Michael House.*
Two walled gardens
are connected to the
house by breezeways.
149. Arrival
elevation.

marble cottages in Newport, Rhode Island, than the Addison Mizner Sea Island cottages that would have surrounded the Glenn residence. Shutze typically included designs for all interior details; here, as was his custom, he also drew the architectural ornament, furniture, lighting fixtures, ceramic bric-a-brac, and wall paintings (*figure 151*). Shutze used elaborate door surrounds and an orchestration of furniture to develop a formal character for all the rooms. An undulating iron seashell motif in the iron balustrade dominates the entrance foyer; it is the most imaginative element in the entire scheme (*figure 152*). Unfortunately, this house remained only a baroque fantasy on paper because Mr. Glenn considered the times too unpredictable to support the construction of a vacation retreat of such splendor.

Although Shutze employed his knowledge of Italian architecture most frequently in residential design, he also created significant public works using a variety of Italian inspirations. In 1928 and 1929, the firm was in large measure occupied with the renovation of the Citizens and Southern National Bank (discussed in chapter 2) and the development of an impressive design for The Temple in Atlanta. The Hebrew Benevolent Congregation needed a larger building, and

150. Proposed Glenn House, elevation.
151. Preliminary presentation drawing of the living room.
152. Entry hall.

151

152

153. Temple of the Hebrew Benevolent Congregation, detail of facade.
154. The design mixes references, with American materials of red brick and stone and classically-derived temple facades.

153

it commissioned Hentz, Adler and Shutze to design a new synagogue and educational building for its present Peachtree Road site. The initial concept was an operatic composition of predominantly Venetian ecclesiastical references, the sort of design Shutze would have termed full-blooded Italian baroque (*figure 155*). The central-planned, domed mass based on Santa Maria della Salute (designed 1631) was approached by way of a projecting temple facade. In a surviving side elevation study, the cupola was drawn as a faceted onion form capped with a tall delicate spike. The materials of this first concept were stucco with wrought iron detailing. Although they decided that this design was too expensive, congregation members familiar with Venice may have found the architectural references too Catholic; however, the proportional system for the design of Santa Maria della Salute is derived from number theory of the Cabala, but it is not known whether Shutze was aware of this historical detail.[24]

By comparison with the first scheme the realized project is modest, and it contains references to American architecture—such as the red brick exterior with stone detailing—that the congregation's building committee considered more appropriate (*figure 154*). The Rabbi David Marx, in particular, helped direct the

124

155

architects in creating a dramatically rich array of symbolic ornament. The interior and exterior contain classical details transformed with Hebrew references (*figure 156*). The decorative program includes unusual altar elements like the two bronze griffins and candelabra that surround the railing which is detailed with triple laurel wreaths flanked by swirling ribbons. The gold-leafed Ark of the Covenant was placed within a dramatic architectural surround composed of a semicircular space with four Ionic columns supporting a curving beam. Athos Menaboni painted these brown scagliola columns and behind them were hung golden curtains suggestive of the tent fabric that surrounded the ancient tabernacle.[25] Centered above the altar area is the traditional eternal light that, in keeping with the Reform congregation's desire to use American imagery, hangs from the eagle and stars in the Great Seal of the United States. The auditorium area becomes a white backdrop for the dramatic altar focus of the design, but Shutze thoroughly enriched this space with symbolic plaster details.[26]

The entry facade is composed of two major temple forms: the upper circular temple which contains the dome lantern, and the entry front, which was developed from Bernini's Sant' Andrea al Quirinale in Rome (1658–70). Here Shutze makes a typical transformation of a precedent. He employed a subordinate order of elements composed within another: at Sant' Andrea a pedimented temple facade surrounds a circular temple supported on two columns that is backed by an arched window. Shutze used each of these elements in The Temple design, but he changed the materials and expanded the single bay of the model to three bays to alter radically the compositional effect of the design. The overall massing creates a strong simple composition: its stone architectural details are imposed on a red brick background; the center curving porch is transformed from pure classicism by traditional Hebrew symbols on the frieze and the crowning tablets which are enveloped in a "tree of life" cartouche (*figure 153*). This crowning element reads more prominently because it is backed by thermal window details. The Temple is sited at a dramatic elevation approximately fifteen feet above the street. Although the building now faces a grass lawn, the original design called for a staircase of increasing width as one approached from the street, a device Shutze was able to realize in other projects. This perspective foreshortening would have made the building's facade even more prominant above Peachtree Road.

Shutze employed a more restrained classical idiom for the Glenn Memorial

155. Shutze's initial, but unbuilt, concept for The Temple is perhaps his only use of the Italian baroque style for a religious building.

156. Temple of Hebrew Benevolent
Congregation, interior. Plaster detailing
references Hebrew themes developed by
Rabbi David Marx.
157. Detail of the altar, showing Holy Ark
flanked by candelabra.

157

Church, which is sited on the periphery of the Emory University campus (*figure 158*). The entry tower owes its general outline to English baroque precedent. Shutze developed the cupola details from the tower of All Saints' Church, Bristol, England. His composition does not reflect a pure reference to a single stylistic period, however, as may be seen in the bold cubic masses and reserved detailing, which are more closely aligned with eighteenth-century French neoclassicism.

158. Glenn Memorial Church is on a natural rise above adjacent streets; access is by a circling drive close to the building.

Of the two significant commissions that Thomas K. Glenn brought to Hentz, Adler and Shutze, only the Glenn Memorial Church was constructed. A powerful force in Atlanta's financial circles, Glenn served as president or chairman of the board of numerous companies.[28] Glenn and his sister Mrs. Charles Howard (Flora) Candler endowed this church as a memorial to their parents—the Reverend Wilbur Fisk Glenn and Florella Glenn. The building functions both as a Methodist church and as Emory University's principal auditorium; to accommodate the 1,500 seats needed for university functions, Shutze made the interior space somewhat wider than might be expected in an ecclesiastical form. And since the choir and altar area must also serve as a performing stage, Shutze hinged its Palladian arch to allow it to swing back to create a clear open space for the stage. Some of Shutze's original decorative features, including this Palladian arch, were removed when the interior was altered recently to provide even more seating.

The Education Building, added in 1939, is separated from the freestanding church by an exterior grassed outdoor theater whose stage and backdrop ornament its west wall (*figure 159*). Unexpressed on the exterior, a chapel of jewel-like delicacy is contained within the Education Building. The Little Chapel (*figures 165, 166*), as Flora Candler named it, developed from the study of a specific precedent, Christopher Wren's St. Stephen, Walbrook, considered one of Wren's finest London churches (*figure 164*). As in earlier examples, Shutze employed the historic structure as a conceptual image, but in this case he studied its unusual spatial and structural organization more than its details.

The building program presented Shutze with a restricted space in which to insert an elaborate chapel. To create a jewel of space as well as ornament, Shutze studied Wren's inventive solution of placing a dome over a traditional nave-and-aisle plan. In his approximately thirty-three foot square chapel, Shutze shaped the appearance of nave and side aisles as Wren had demonstrated by using a shallow dome over the nave and lowering the ceiling over what were effectively

159

160

159. *Education Building, Glenn Memorial Church. Outdoor theater with stepping grassed terraces and stage.*
160. *The rear wall of Glenn Memorial Church faces the outdoor theater.*
161. *Entry facade with view of outdoor theater to left. The Little Chapel occupies the two-story space to the right of the entry; the right chimney is false and disguises the chapel's light monitor.*

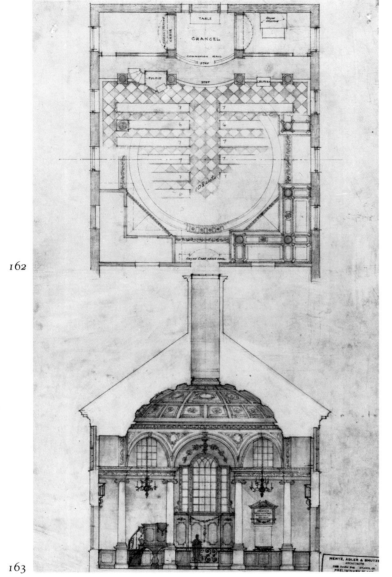

162

163

162. *Little Chapel, Education Building, Glenn Memorial Church. Initial plan and partial reflected ceiling.*

163. *Initial section. The final design deleted the pulpit and placed the organ console and pipes at the front of the church; the false chimney is actually a light monitor.*

164. *St. Stephen, Walbrook, London, designed by Christopher Wren, engraving. For the Little Chapel, Shutze employed Wren's structural concept of supporting a dome on arches springing from eight free-standing columns.*

side aisles. In both designs, a square is defined within the flowing space of the plan by twelve freestanding columns; they support eight arches upon which rests the base of a coffered dome.

Shutze detailed and proportioned the chapel in a similar manner to the seventeenth-century church using details such as columns raised on plinths that allowed unobstructed views of the full column length. For his columns, Wren employed the Corinthian order, but Shutze, for his much more intimate space, selected the simpler Ionic order. Wren placed an unusual series of oval windows along the length of St. Stephen's side walls; so did Shutze in his chapel's entry

164

wall (*figure 166*). These windows are striking elements in each of the designs.

The exquisite quality of the chapel's ornament expresses the coordinated efforts of Shutze and H. J. Millard, the designer and the craftsman. Native southern flowers served as models for new forms of classically detailed garlands and friezes (*figure 165*). Only the entry surround recalls St. Stephen with its contrasting dark oak against white plaster walls. The realized door with its exceptional detailing did not depend on St. Stephen, but a preliminary design with organ pipes crowning the door composition was derived from the main entrance to Wren's church.

165. *Little Chapel, Education Building, Glenn Memorial Church, interior view toward altar. The original design used clear glass window above the altar.*
166. *Interior view toward entry. Herbert Millard carved the chapel's ornament, including the intricately detailed entry door surround.*

*167. Ferst House,
view toward the entry
court.
168. Elevation.
169. First floor plan,
showing irregular
massing, which is
unusual in Shutze's
designs.*

Shutze's stylistic preferences lay first of all in Italian architecture ranging in period from Roman to baroque. His second interest included classical styles from England—the baroque of Wren, eighteenth-century neoclassical, and Regency of the nineteenth century. His interest in American precedent first appears in his work in the 1930s and continues into his last realized designs of the 1950s. He was least interested in the vernacular forms of France and England. He had traveled in France and England while he was a student at the American Academy in Rome and, as the results indicate, he designed with assurance in any historical style he selected. French architecture as a design precedent is extremely rare in Shutze's work perhaps because he developed an intense distaste for the Beaux-Arts system; this attitude may have colored his stylistic selections, or it may merely reflect the preferences of his clients.

For the Monie Ferst house of 1929 Shutze looked to French vernacular architecture and especially to farmhouses in Normandy (*figure 167*). The vernacular and picturesque forms of this region occur with increasing frequency in American architecture following the exposure of many Americans to that portion of France during World War I. Shutze's Ferst house compares stylistically with contemporary work by the Philadelphia firm of Mellor, Meigs, and Howe. Shutze matched his landscaping to the romantically unpretentious rural spirit of the Ferst house by placing it deep in a virgin wood approached on axis through the untouched natural setting. The house partially surrounds a walled courtyard on three sides with an irregularly shaped one- and two-story building, slate hipped roofs, and walls projecting into gable dormers. The garage is topped with a multilevel dovecote and the ell of the house turns on a cylindrical stair tower. Within, diagonal axes connect the principal rooms to the entry hall (*figure 169*). The materials are stone and white-painted brick. Shutze created as successful a rendition of the Normandy farmhouse as any other contemporary architect and yet it may be his only design in the style.

Shutze produced a variety of appearances using English precedent. The Charles Nunnally house is a formal design developed from English Renaissance architecture. The firm invested a great deal of time designing this project, as Shutze's numerous sketches reveal the meticulous process of design study. Un-

167

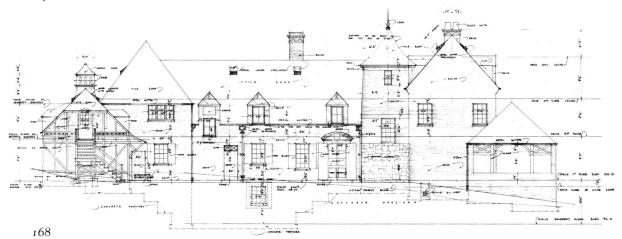

168

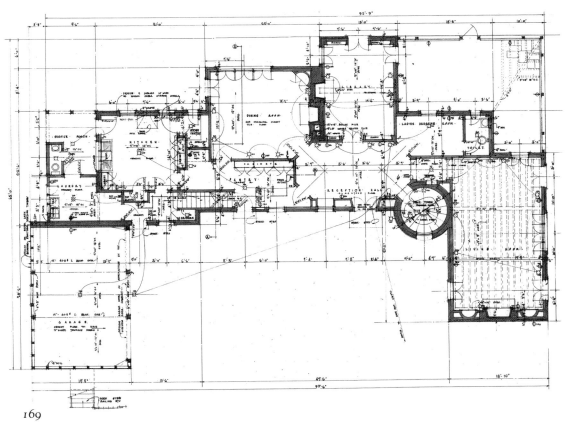

169

170

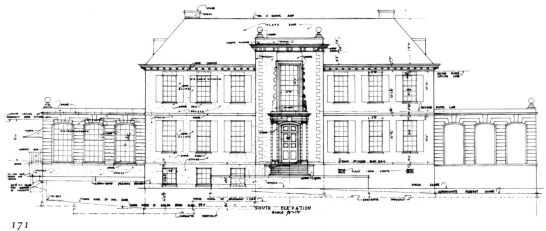

170. *Nunnally House, project, unbuilt,
interior sketch by Shutze.*
171. *Elevation, taken from the working
drawings.*

172. Stout House, Chicago, was the childhood home of Eleanor Stout McRae, and provided the stylistic inspiration for the McRae house in Atlanta (figures 173– 180).

fortunately Charles Nunnally died in 1932, a few months after completion of the working drawings, and the house, designed for a West Paces Ferry site, was never realized (*figures 170, 171*).

The irregular massing of an English manor house served as the image for the residence of Dr. and Mrs. Floyd McRae (*figure 173*), designed from 1927 to 1929. The client and principal source of inspiration for the McRae house on Habersham Road was Eleanor McRae, by all accounts an intriguing woman. One of the first women in Georgia to receive an airplane pilot's license, she was also active in Atlanta's civic affairs. Her husband was for many years the chief of staff at Piedmont Hospital. Mrs. McRae selected an architectural style reminiscent of her childhood home on Lakeshore Drive in Chicago (*figure 172*). Many of Shutze's rich interior details for the living and dining rooms ultimately were omitted because Mrs. McRae felt she no longer needed to live with the architectural splendor she had known as a child; however, she did maintain for her husband and child a standard of living that required the assistance of a staff of eight to ten servants.

The parti for many of Shutze's houses included an entry foyer with a staircase rising in a graceful curve across the wall faced on entering the house (*figure 176*). The McRae house employs this device, but the ascending stair wall is penetrated by a doorway leading down to the breakfast room and visually leading out to the garden. The foyer receives little natural light, so the bright east-facing mullioned glass wall and delicate columns that support a shallow saucer dome in the breakfast room draw attention through and out into the landscape (*figure 178*).

Unlike most of Shutze's residential work, the McRae house has an irregular picturesque massing in its principal facade; however, on the garden facade, an L-shaped plan created by the loggia connection between the garage/servants' quarters and the main house produces both highly irregular and, when viewed on axis, rigidly symmetrical images (*figure 179*). On the foyer-breakfast room axis, the garden facade is a powerful symmetrical mass, but in non-axial views, the irregularities of building mass and garden terraces create a romantic image allied with the general character of the building.

Many of Shutze's residential designs are conceived as architectural backdrops for gardens. Such is the case with his design for the garage/servants' quarters of the McRae house, which incorporate a two-story stone wall with dovecote and marble doves fitted into the gable end (*figure 180*). This decorated wall serves as an architectural backdrop for the lower garden terrace. The ultimate garden element is the finest doghouse in Atlanta. Built of stucco walls with a slate gable roof, this structure served as the home of the family's large German shepherd, Baron Von Richtofen, known affectionately as Ricky.

In the same period Shutze employed similar irregular massing for the Spring Hill Mortuary, which was designed for H. M. Patterson and Sons in 1927–28 (*figure 181*). The Spring Hill design contrasts interior and exterior detailing: English manor houses provide the general external imagery, and delicate English baroque white stucco work decorates the principal chapel (*figure 183*). H. M. Patterson introduced the innovative concept of a mortuary home to Atlanta; he wanted to move his establishment from its urban storefront location to the practically suburban location of Spring and 10th Streets. Shutze provided the intimate homelike atmosphere of the new mortuary, the variety of whose masses, details, and roof planes created a picturesque outline in keeping with the desired effect of the building. Shutze specified an inexpensive grade of paint to provide a thin wash of white over the brick walls with the desire that it would rapidly disappear and produce an impression of age by its subtle patina. He also called for vines to be trained to grow on the building to further enhance the sense of created history.[29]

173

174

173. McRae House. Although Shutze seldom evoked images of the English manor house, he did here, taking inspiration from a precedent in Chicago (figure 172).
174. Gates adjacent to the house.
175. Side entrance.

177

178

*176. McRae House, main entry hall looking
toward side entry.*
177. Side entry hall.
178. Breakfast room.

179. McRae House, axial view of the garden facade; the breakfast room is in the center of the elevation.
180. Garage and servants' quarters, seen from the upper terrace.

180

181

182

183

IV

In the 1920s while Shutze was realizing his finest Italian baroque work, he began to explore more reserved forms of classicism. His first use of English Regency probably dates to 1924 with the Dismukes house in Columbus, Georgia, that he designed for Hentz, Reid and Adler.[30] His choice at this time to study English neoclassicism, English Regency, and the work of John Soane (1753–1837) may have been influenced by a desire to accommodate current aesthetic interests in simplicity of detailing and geometric massing. Shutze never produced a residence in the popular modern idioms of art deco, streamlined modern, or the international style, but his selection of particular eighteenth- and nineteenth-century forms of classicism may have been his response to modern aesthetics.

In 1929 Shutze designed the Harry L. English and J. J. Goodrum houses in the English Regency style (*figures 184, 186*). Although the two houses differ in appearance, they share numerous common features: planar walls painted light cream or white, a spare use of ornament, and symmetrical outline. Shutze developed these and other individual characteristics—such as elongated columns, bow windows, wrought iron railings, metal canopies, and Gothic detailing—from English Regency models. The Goodrum house, designed for the recently widowed May Goodrum, was a more elaborate concept than the Harry English house. The principal interior feature of each house, however, was a dining room with Oriental details. The current owner of the English house, Anne Cox-Chambers, a former ambassador to Belgium, has preserved the original details of the dining room, which is the most exceptional room in the house (*figure 185*). For this room, Shutze created classicized Oriental details. Curving broken pediments stand in relief before niches that hold porcelain Chinese figures. The delicate spirit of the room is enhanced with Chinese wallpaper, mirror overmantle, and crystal chandelier.

Mrs. James J. Goodrum, born May Patterson, gave Shutze the Goodrum house commission. Remembered as an exquisite lady of great refinement, May Goodrum was an exceptionally important client. She gave him other design projects including her Sea Island house, and undoubtedly was influential in his receiving the commission for the Rabun Gap-Nacoochee School, which she helped organize. Unlike most of Shutze's clients, she was not born to wealth,

181. Spring Hill Mortuary was cleaned recently of vines and repainted, altering Shutze's creation of an "aged" appearance of the building.
182. Detail of the chapel ceiling.
183. Interior of the chapel, looking toward the altar.

184. English House
was based on English
Regency models.

185. The dining room
is in the Chinese
Chippendale style,
which was very
popular during the
Regency period.

186

187

186. Goodrum
House, which was
originally painted with
a thin wash of
mustard yellow over
its brick walls, was
accented with apple
green shutters in
keeping with Regency
taste.
187. Detail of the
arrival elevation.

and at the time of her marriage to a prominent Atlanta businessman, she sold cosmetics at Jacob's Drug Store. This match had lasted only two years when Mr. Goodrum died in June 1928; yet, by August 1929, drawings had been prepared by Shutze's firm for a house with extensive gardens. Shutze decided to use the English Regency instead of his preferred Italian baroque for its characteristic mix of classicism with exotic details (here, Gothic and Oriental). The entry and garden facades are reserved, balanced, and originally enlivened with mustard yellow walls and bright apple green shutters.

Shutze's interior detailing required the combined artistry of his most talented colleagues. For the decoration of the octagonal breakfast room, Shutze gave complete design freedom to Athos Menaboni, who painted the ceiling's ogee curved vault illusionistically as an openwork trellis with birds and vines (*figure 198*). For the wall niches, Menaboni painted humorous scenes of domestic life featuring Oriental figures, flora, and fauna. He surrounded the figures with 18 karat gold paint to produce a luminous quality of light within the room. Allyn Cox painted the dining room mural on canvas in his studio and shipped it to Atlanta for installation (*figures 190, 192*). The concept of the mural comes from

189

the Royal Pavilion at Brighton, England (1815–21) which combines Oriental and Arabic details to produce one of the world's most exotic buildings. Cox designed a parade of Americanized Oriental figures that focus their attention on a Buddha from Thailand, who sits impassively on a cushion above the fireplace. Other plaster and painted detailing in the room was completed by Menaboni.

H. J. Millard carved the woodwork in the living room and entry hall (*figures 194, 195*). Shutze designed floral swags of native southern flowers for the door surrounds in the living room in perfect representations of hibiscus, magnolias, sunflowers, camellias, roses, and morning glories. The fireplace surround and entry stair decoration are rococo compositions of floral elements with rivulets of water pouring from cornucopia. The single modern note in all the lush interior details is the delicate openwork of the stair railing, which has a vaguely modernized Chinese Chippendale appearance (*figure 195*). In total, the detailing is a robust display of collaborative artistry, and for their efforts the firm received the award of merit from the New York Architectural League in 1932.

Shutze also landscaped the Goodrum residence with enormous care (*figure 196*). He enclosed the estate in a brick and wrought iron fence accented at

190. *Goodrum House, like the English house (figure 185), has interiors in the Chinese Chippendale style; the dining room mural was painted by Allyn Cox, while the ceiling, cornice, and base details were painted by Athos Menaboni.*
191. *Entry hall looking into dining room.*

190

192. *Detail of dining room mural.*
193. *Dining room, looking through the stair hall into the living room.*
194. *Herbert Millard's carving is above the living room door.*
195. *Detail of the entry hall balustrade.*

191

192

193

194

195

196. Goodrum House, site plan published in A Garden History of Georgia (drawing not by Shutze). In addition to the garden theater, oriental and gothic camellia house, and bowling green illustrated here, Shutze also designed a boxwood maze shaped in the initials of May Patterson Goodrum. 197. The bowling green and exotic garden folly.

Plan of the Garden of
MRS JAMES J GOODRUM
ATLANTA GEORGIA.

197

intervals with Gothic arched openings filled with English geometric iron tracery. Like the gardens at the Inman house, the Goodrum gardens were meant to be primarily green with numerous boxwoods and grass lawns. Using a concept he would have learned from the Villa Gori near Siena, Shutze surrounded the house with garden elements such as a garden theater, the stage of which was defined by hedges.[31] Shutze placed a Chinese camellia house with Gothic details on the axis of the rear or garden facade of the house. And, to the west side of the garden facade, he surrounded a lawn bowling green with serpentine walls like those created by Thomas Jefferson for the University of Virginia. This bowling green terminates with a folly shaped like a Hindu howdah and is surmounted by an eagle (*figure 197*). In the front yard, Shutze later added a boxwood maze developed from May Patterson Goodrum's initials.

159

In 1928 and 1929 Shutze designed the Standard Club, an exclusive social organization then located on Ponce de Leon Avenue in Atlanta (*figures 199, 200*). Again, Shutze turned to nineteenth-century English Regency details with planar brick walls, a six-columned Ionic portico, and a particularly severe treatment of moldings and window heads. The ballroom, the principal interior space, was treated in a lighthearted manner with delicate stucco work, a vaulted ceiling, and a range of columns in front of the long walls of the rectangular space. In his renderings, Shutze enhanced the character of this room even further by including sphinxes to ornament the entry to the ballroom. Such dramatic contrast between plain exterior detailing and exuberant, but delicate interior treatment may frequently be found in Shutze's work. This excellent example of an American adaptation of the English Regency style burned completely in 1963.

Two residences designed in 1936 provide further evidence of Shutze's adaptation of classical tradition to modern aesthetics in the style he had established in the Goodrum residence. The Ben Smith house in Atlanta has been mistakenly identified from the distant street as an international style design; however, upon close inspection the house reveals its true identity as an English Regency design with an upper level room streamlined in its curving end walls (*figure 201*). Shutze's clients were newly married twenty-two-year-olds and his first design for them was in the Italian baroque. Perhaps adhering to current taste, the young clients rejected the design as too formal for their life-style and the only remains of this original scheme are the sweeping stucco entry gates.

The couple accepted Shutze's third scheme, which is the constructed English Regency design, the masonry walls of which are painted in pristine white. As in the Goodrum house, Shutze employed geometric forms that here become powerful cubic masses relieved by the curving walls of the penthouse and the entry porches. His porches are circular and bow in plan surrounded by fluted Doric columns made of concrete.

The interior continues the design's sense of serenity with an entry hall almost abstract in its clean lines with smooth plaster walls recessed in arched coves around doorways (*figure 202*). The most peculiarly modern detail of the design is the so-called penthouse, which resulted from a programmatic demand for an observation area (*figure 204*). The curving end walls are filled with glass windows and paired doors that open onto roof terraces. The nautical flavor of the room

199

199. *Standard Club, another use by Shutze
of English Regency details.*
200. *The ballroom is the principal space,
lighthearted with delicate stucco work on the
ceiling.*

201

*201. Smith House, garden elevation facing
street. The lower, Regency-detailed geometric
masses are surmounted by an observation
room with curving end walls.*
202. Entry hall seen from the living room.

204

and its terraces is enhanced by a curving bar, which sits on a raised platform and has the appearance of a ship's helm. The room's character fits with the stylish interiors of the 1930s American avant-garde, but Shutze subdued its appearance from temporary voguishness to the more timeless qualities of his tradition. The exterior details of the curving penthouse are rendered in concert with the lower Regency detailed building masses through regularly spaced Doric pilasters.

A second design that owes its austere character to the legacy of the Goodrum house was the residence of Dan Conklin on Blackland Road (*figure 205*). Like the Goodrum and Smith houses, rough brick walls painted white give the general impression of severe geometry. The triadic arrangement of the principal elements focuses on a simple massive cube which is matched on either side by smaller cubes linked with covered columned passageways (*figure 206*). The detailing was developed from Shutze's study of John Soane, with the small side masses being especially reminiscent of the Dulwich Picture Gallery. The interiors continue the severe character of the exterior with moldings of simple geometric lines, smooth plaster walls, and a gracefully curving stair that rises from the foyer. The dining room projects outward from the main mass of the house as a semicircular ended

167

element. Its gib windows pocket overhead, and the door openings thereby created transform the room into an open flowing space. As in the Smith house, Shutze gave the playroom a modern character. Wall murals by Athos Menaboni, which include light figures suspended within dark wall surfaces, and a curving bar create a stylistic counterpoint to the formal classicism of the other public rooms (*figure 207*).

205. Conklin House. The English Regency style, especially the work of John Soane, provided Shutze with classical precedents from which reserved geometric designs could develop.
206. Detail of front elevation.
207. Playroom with mural by Athos Menaboni.

From 1920 to 1936 Shutze introduced enormous stylistic variety to his work, but whenever the opportunity arose, he returned to the Italian baroque as the inspiration for his designs. From 1927 to 1935, Hentz, Adler and Shutze received approximately 100 commissions that ranged from small renovations to major institutional, religious, residential, and educational buildings. The severe economic conditions of the depression seem to have had no immediate effect upon the firm's clientele; by 1932, however, the number of commissions began to decline, and by the following year prospects for work had grown sufficiently alarming that the partners agreed to take no salaries for the year. In 1934 the same procedure was followed; however, in 1935 the firm's work began to increase, and the following year it tripled. This abundance of projects continued until Shutze retired from full-time practice. Economic trends improved, and the firm of Hentz, Adler and Shutze changed in turn.

In 1936, Warren Armistead became an associate of the firm, and with him came the firm's most significant repeat clients. Armistead had worked previously for Marye, Alger and Venour, the architects of Atlanta's Fox Theater. This firm had a number of Southern Bell Telephone and Telegraph projects, and because Armistead had made sufficiently close contacts with the clients he was offered the work if he could associate with an established architectural firm. Since Hentz, Adler and Shutze had the foremost reputation in Atlanta, Armistead presented them with the prospect of additional work in the very lean 1930s; they accepted his proposal.[32] However, Armistead's name would not be added to this firm until 1944, first as Shutze, Armistead and Adler, and the following year, upon the death of Rudolph Adler, as Shutze and Armistead. This partnership represented Shutze's last professional association, and upon their agreement to terminate this business relationship in 1950, Shutze practiced by himself. The work brought to the firm by Armistead initiated a new phase in Shutze's career, one for which his training may not have fully prepared him.

205

206

207

208. *Thornton House.*

IV
THE CLASSICAL TRADITION IN THE
MODERN PERIOD

209. Philip Trammell Shutze, ca. 1940.

The final phase of Shutze's most active professional life—the years of his association with Warren Armistead—dates from 1936 to 1950. It was a period characterized both by dramatic changes within the firm and great continuity in Shutze's personal practice of architecture. Through Armistead's influence, the firm's clientele included for the first time major corporate clients, who were as much, if not more, concerned with costs as they were with the aesthetic images that their architecture projected. Despite a staggering number of commissions, Shutze refused to alter the design approach that had proven so appropriate in the past. His attitude met resistance within the firm. Quite unwillingly on Shutze's part, the focus of his office changed along with its clientele: the business of architecture began to conflict with the aesthetics of design.

During this last decade and a half of Shutze's partnership in a large office, he created numerous highly-acclaimed buildings, principally for institutions. With the economic problems of the depression, fewer wealthy Atlantans sought Shutze's expensive expertise in residential design. He also produced hundreds of utilitarian buildings with the same floor plan; for these he designed individualized elevations appropriate to their contexts. Unlike so many architects who would have considered such projects merely lucrative work, Shutze treated them as opportunities to study classical design solutions for cities and towns across the Southeast.

By 1936 the depression's impact upon the construction industry had begun to lessen, and with the Southern Bell Telephone and Telegraph jobs provided by Warren Armistead, the firm prospered once again. During the depression, however, modern aesthetics had begun to dominate architectural education and design. Shutze had little interest in the new severe style, and he did not introduce the image of modernism into his designs. He used a few streamlined elements, but only for bars and playrooms—places for incidental social activities and therefore appropriately designed in what he may have considered popular and transitory styles. Shutze did, however, modify his classicism; as in the Goodrum house of 1930, he found that English Regency architecture offered an appropriate precedent for modern aesthetic requirements.[1] In 1936 Shutze employed the Regency style in residential commissions for Dan Conklin, Albert E. Thornton (*figure 208*), and Ben T. Smith. Each design employed masonry, either painted brick or stucco, to accent severe geometric massing. These Regency designs should not be regarded as part of an evolutionary sequence in Shutze's work; rather, they demonstrate

210. Goodrum Sea Island House.

the inclusiveness of Shutze's classicism, which accommodated an aesthetic otherwise antithetical to his own beliefs.

As commissions increased dramatically, Shutze had ample opportunities to vary his classicism in response to his clients' needs. May Goodrum commissioned Shutze to design a beach cottage at Sea Island, Georgia (*figure 210*). For this lighthearted design, Shutze selected the stucco architecture of Bermuda as his design precedent. Sea Island's architectural style had been established by Addison Mizner (1872–1933), the prolific Palm Beach architect of the wealthy, who designed the Cloisters, the island's only hotel, as well as a number of residences. Shutze did not feel constrained by this local precedent, and he found "island resort architecture" more appropriate for his project. This new model employed the canted walls and the peculiarly Bermuda-esque stepped roof, which effectively break from Mizner's use of Spanish precedent. For interior and exterior detailing, Shutze used a scallop shell motif to refer symbolically to the seaside location.

In the late 1930s, when residential work comprised a smaller portion of the firm's work, the firm continued to produce at least one significant residential project each year. Shutze received a second commission from Fred Patterson in

211. Patterson-Carr House. The irregular massing is seen well from a distant street.

212. Access to the house is from within the walled garden.

213. A louvered door gives access to an open gallery that borders the walled garden.

212

213

214

215

214. Shutze dramatized the arrival to the house in its rural setting by alternating the sequence of public/open with private/enclosed spaces.

215. A garden is formed by the irregular massing of the house.

1939 for an enlarged version of the original 1933 house on Habersham Road (*figure 211*). Based on eighteenth-century American vernacular precedent, the design differs stylistically from the Spring Hill Mortuary built a decade earlier for H. M. Patterson. However, with their picturesque, irregular compositions, each breaks with the dominant strains of classicism that more typically characterize Shutze's work.

For the Patterson-Carr house, Shutze developed a third and essentially American association of house to landscape. The earlier house-landscape arrangements that dominate his work evolved either from Italian villas or from formal English or American models. In the villa model, Shutze places the house on the sloping landscape where its theatrical facade faces the public thoroughfare and the formal approach drive; its arrival point occurs, however, at the rear of the building. The Calhoun, Inman, and Smith houses exemplify this arrangement. In the second model, whether with an English or American precedent, Shutze makes the house an independent object connected to the public view by an axis, which terminates in an entry court immediately in front of a symmetrical facade. The axis typically extends through the house and into the gardens that frame the rear facade. In the third model, Shutze places the house within the landscape with little acknowledgement of its connection to the public thoroughfare.

Shutze placed the Patterson-Carr house at a distance from the road and created an entry sequence appropriate to its picturesque nature (*figure 212*). Between white rail fences bordered by an avenue of Japanese Kwansan cherry trees, a lengthy driveway runs alongside the point of entry. In keeping with the asymmetry of the design, Shutze first presents the visitor with an external door of patterned louvers placed within the extended gable brick facade, the edge of which descends to form the garden's encircling wall. Originally a large oak shaded half the garden—a grass lawn surrounded by brick paths and flower beds. The walled garden opens to the cool shade of a roofed gallery, and the gallery protects the entry door proper. With this entry sequence Shutze disconnected the house and the street and made the absence of axiality into an uncharacteristically forceful compositional element. The power of the arrangement derives from placing an urban garden form in a rural landscape; the walled garden humanizes a part of nature much as Shutze's classicist interior details humanize his interior spaces.

The interior of the house is informally arranged with major rooms opening through window vistas, or French doors, to the surrounding intimate gardens. Appropriate to the scale of the house, these are intimately scaled flower gardens of various sizes formed by the architectural massing of the house; they are extended or enclosed by garden walls (*figure 215*).

In addition to the opulent residential work for which his office was recognized, Shutze also designed a low income housing project. Atlanta was in the forefront of government-subsidized low-income housing with the construction of Techwood Homes, the first such project in America. In 1936, the same year Techwood was dedicated, Shutze and a number of other architects collaborated on the design of Clark Howell Homes on Lucky Street at North Avenue, adjacent to Techwood Homes (*figure 217*).[2]

The earlier Techwood Homes project presented a modern appearance with its flat roofs, metal casement windows, and massive rectangular blocks, details that were demanded by the governmental advisers, according to Preston Stevens, Sr., one of Techwood's architects. However, Shutze approached this modern housing type like all of his work, by building upon tradition, rather than relying on new appearances in vogue at the moment. Shutze created a village of housing around a playing field, and a civic activity center of library and recreation buildings.

The plan and the architectural details break from the monotony that has characterized so many attempts at government housing. Shutze and his colleagues employed details like fenced front and back yards and varied door surrounds and door colors to give individuality to the units (*figures 216, 218*). As forcefully symbolic as the modernists' use of flat roofs, Clark Howell Homes' gable roofs conveyed a traditional image to the new housing type. Today, Clark Howell appears in better condition than many projects in the Atlanta area, which one supposes are similarly administered and maintained.

Shutze's only major work that could be termed stylistically modern employed in its inception an eighteenth-century artistic concept. In 1938 he designed the Mirador Room for the Capital City Club, a private men's club in Atlanta's urban business district (*figure 219*). The club, of which Shutze was a member, decided to convert the existing ballroom into a more intimate dining and dancing facility, comparable to the supper clubs then popular in New York City.[3] In keeping with his earlier designs for residential bars and playrooms, Shutze shaped the room

216

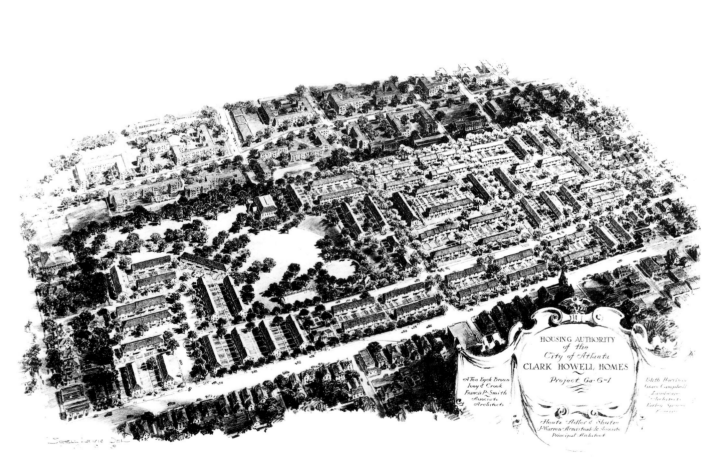

217

218

216. Clark Howell
Homes, proposed
building elevation with
color alternatives to
personalize buildings.
217. Site plan.
218. Proposed
building elevation.

with the curves and countercurves of the streamlined modern style. The most noteworthy element of the design is its mirrored walls, from which the name Mirador Room derived. He employed mirrors to achieve a sense of openness and light in a room centered within the building and therefore cut off from natural light. He had been fascinated with eighteenth-century Chinese reverse mirror painting and he seized this opportunity to experiment with his interest. This form of painting had the practical advantage of protecting the painted surface while allowing the exposed glass surface to be cleaned.

Shutze engaged Athos Menaboni to design and produce the panels, but first Menaboni had to rediscover the design principles involved in this lost art. Painting on the back of the glass panels required the application of the painting's finishing touches first, followed by layers and tones in the reverse of their normal order.[4] Menaboni tried to paint by looking at his work in a mirror, but he found this impossible. Instead, he had continuously to walk around to the panel's finished surface to check the positive image as it developed. After this tedious process was completed, the painted surfaces were washed with mirror silver. Menaboni based his designs on flora and fauna native to Georgia and he created compositions of birds and tree limbs for each panel.

179

219. *Mirador Room, Capital City Club. The murals were painted by Athos Menaboni; furnishings and ceiling details were later modifications.*

In the early 1940s Shutze received two of his finest design commissions in public architecture. These fully engaged his great design talents, which were not being entirely challenged by the utilitarian projects that comprised the majority of the office's current work. The Fulton County Medical Society Building (later called the Academy of Medicine), and the Whitehead Memorial Room and other additions at the Emory University Hospital are exceptionally late examples of American classical architecture, and not at all in keeping with the modernist or international style of architecture then popular in America (*figures 222, 227*).

Initially, the Academy of Medicine was the project of another Atlanta architect, R. Kennon Perry, and this convoluted business relationship has led to some confusion over the authorship of the design. Perry's difficulties with the project began when he produced a modern design scheme. Dr. Phinizy Calhoun, the brother of Andrew Calhoun for whom the firm of Hentz, Reid and Adler in 1923 had designed the Italian baroque Calhoun house, was on the Academy's building committee; he decided that Shutze would be a more appropriate architect for the job and took his proposal to Shutze. Recognizing that changing architects after a project has begun could be a delicate matter, Shutze carefully explored the situation with Perry. The new contract clearly stated each architect's responsibilities: Perry maintained his position as principal architect in charge of working drawings and supervision, Shutze would design the building.[5]

The Academy of Medicine functioned as a meeting place for medical practitioners and as a central medical library. For the design Shutze related that he looked to the Medical College of Georgia in Augusta (ca. 1835) for a precedent (*figure 223*). The Medical College is a federal-style building, the American equivalent of the English Regency style. Although it bears little resemblance to Shutze's design, each building is characterized by an entry portico, severely detailed stucco walls, and a general feeling of reserve. The Academy also evokes the imagery of Russian neoclassical architecture. The aesthetic power of the exterior depends on its simple and severe lines: the base is marked with linear rustication; wall masses terminate in plain pilasters; and round-headed windows are set within undetailed surrounds. The severity of the design highlights an unfluted six-columned Doric entry portico, the impact of which is further reinforced by a square tower containing coffered semicircular skylights. The single side entrance (*figure 220*) is an equally reserved arrangement, with two unfluted Doric columns in antis similar in composition to the main entry and stairs of the Scarbrough house (1819) in Savannah. The designer of that house, William Jay, was an Englishman whose style reflected the characteristics of his countryman and contemporary John Soane. Shutze therefore adapted the work of two Regency architects—one in England and one in America.

From these main and side entry points, hallways converge in front of an auditorium and beneath a domed, skylighted foyer (*figure 224*). Developed from a study of the Old Dividend Office (1818–23) in John Soane's Bank of England in London, Shutze's details in the foyer feature pilasters extending into linear moldings that accent arches, a shallow saucer dome pierced with a clerestory, and a caduceus ornament. This important ornament, the symbol of Hermes and Aesclepius, seems appropriate to a medical organization, but its less well-known association with Mercury as the messenger carrying information between man and the gods makes it equally appropriate to Soane's bank.[6] Because the United States Army Medical Corps had recently chosen the caduceus as its insignia, Dr. Howard Haley suggested that it be used at the Academy.[7]

Shutze's use of columns in antis and curving walls supporting semidomes is

220. Academy of Medicine (originally the
Fulton County Medical Society). Side entry
and curving outline of auditorium.
221. Balustrade detail of side entry.
222. Entry facade.

220

221

223. Medical College of Georgia. Shutze looked to this building in Augusta, of ca. 1835, as precedent for his Academy of Medicine.

reminiscent of the English neoclassical architect Robert Adam's handling of such elements, but his generally severe treatment of details evokes the spirit of John Soane's designs. The original coloration was white on the interior and a delicate ochre on the exterior. The building is located in an area of increasing land values and was saved from demolition by a determined group of doctors' wives who recognized its significance. In 1980 the entire building was renovated and partially restored, but Shutze, then ninety years old, was not consulted. The interiors have been redecorated and the sparkling clarity of the original white coloration, which Shutze developed from his study of John Soane's public architecture, particularly his Bank of England, is no longer in evidence.[8]

Shutze's other great public commission of the early 1940s, the Emory University Hospital extension (*figure 226*), expressed his continuing admiration for both English and Italian baroque architecture.[9] The original hospital dated from 1922 and was the work of the firm of Hentz, Reid and Adler; the building expansion was the result of a bequest made by Mrs. Lettie Pate Whitehead Evans as a memorial to her son Conkey Pate Whitehead, who had attended Emory, and to the Whitehead family in general.[10] This new addition consisted of three

224. Academy of Medicine. In the interior, looking toward the side entry, the auditorium is to the right and the main entry is to the left within the semidomed apse.

wings—the entrance, surgical, and service wings—and within the entrance wing, the Whitehead Memorial Room.

The five-story hospital sits on a two-story rusticated base, and its design conveys an Italian Renaissance character through a subdued use of classical detailing on stucco walls. Shutze gave the large building a sense of accessible scale by recessing the side wings and projecting the center pavilion five bays forward; he left the side wings undetailed, and they act as mere backdrops to the center action. The central building mass contains the entry, which is the most highly detailed element in the facade (*figure 225*). The entry doors are recessed beneath a surround of Tuscan columns supporting a broken pediment into which Shutze slipped a second-story window. This window and broken pediment arrangement often characterize a Shutze entrance. To either side of this composition are heavily rusticated and balconied windows with sixteen-over-sixteen lights. These entry elements convey a restrained mannerist character.

Inside the hospital, a spacious classically detailed lobby is presented with amicable formality. In 1948 such a space was becoming rare, especially in the scientifically oriented realm of a hospital. Here the warmth of humanist archi-

226

225. Emory
University Hospital.
The entrance stairs
are recessed within
classically detailed
surround.
226. Entry elevation.

tecture provides a welcome transition for visitors and patients alike. At the end
of a corridor devoted solely to hospital administration is the masterpiece of Shutze's
efforts in this building, the Whitehead Memorial Room (*figure 227*). This room
serves as both the hospital's boardroom and as a shrine housing memorabilia of
the Whitehead family. Shutze and the master woodcarver H. J. Millard collaborated in the design, and they took as their model the work by Christopher Wren
and his master woodcarver Grinling Gibbons. After Millard reviewed Shutze's
designs, he estimated the woodcarving would require over two years of his time
(it actually took three years). In addition he believed the designs were too intricate
to produce in his studio in Cincinnati, Ohio, and ship to the site. To insure that
the project received appropriate care, Millard moved his family to Atlanta from
their home of thirty years.

The most significant elements within the room are four individual portraits
of family members accented by elaborately carved surrounds. The portraits of
Mrs. Evans (*figure 228*) and the senior Joseph Whitehead face each other across
the length of the room; portraits of their sons Conkey Pate and Joseph, Jr., are
between them. Each portrait is enclosed within a cut back three-dimensional

186

227

228

229

227. Whitehead
Memorial Room,
Emory University
Hospital. Herbert
Millard devoted three
years to the carving of
the room's ornament.
228. The portrait of
Mrs. Lettie Pate
Whitehead Evans, the
hospital's benefactress,
hangs within a carved
linden wood frame
representative of
spring.
229. Detail of entry
door.

frame and surmounted by a garland representing one of the four seasons. Mrs. Evans's garland depicts Spring in beribboned swags that support clusters of the season's fruit and flowers, and are crowned by two intertwined birds, one of which gestures toward the portrait of her son Conkey Pate. In a similarly representational composition, Mr. Whitehead's portrait garland depicts Winter, and his sons' portrait garlands portray Summer and Autumn. These magnificent displays of carved linden wood are placed against simple oak-paneled walls. An additional wall decoration worthy of note is an Ionic columned door surround whose broken pediment houses a rampant eagle bedecked with garlands and supporting a wreath framing the family's initials (*figure 229*).

The ceiling, another display of ornate artistry, boasts a heavy, almost massive, presentation of plaster fruit, flowers, seashells, and intertwined initials of the four family members. Although the room is residential in size and contains a lengthy dining room table, the intense quality of the ornament produces a recognizable civic grandeur that distinguishes it from Shutze's residential work. His deft ability to manipulate detailing to create not only an exceptional composition, but that also acknowledges building type, indicates the sureness of his creative control.

In 1947 and 1948 Shutze and Millard also collaborated on the Julian Hightower residence in Thomaston, Georgia (*figure 230*). Shutze and the Hightowers had a longstanding friendship and he was the only architect considered to design their home. Design discussions between client and architect began around 1940, but the turmoil of World War II delayed any substantial work. By the end of the war, the undulating edge of their eighty-acre man-made lake had taken final shape and, after carefully considering several alternatives, Shutze and the Hightowers selected a site on a knoll above a crook in the lake.

The entrance to the site is first marked by brick walls adorned with stone pineapples and wrought iron gates. The driveway takes an undulating path to a circular arrival in front of a two-story temple portico. The clients admired President James Madison's Montpelier (ca. 1755, 1797–1800, 1809–12, 1900) in Orange County, Virginia, and requested that Shutze develop this precedent for their main facade.

Beneath the portico, stairs lead to a four-foot wide mahogany entry door, the size of which forecasts the opulent scale of the interior. A twelve-foot wide foyer with staircase runs the width of the house and, in traditional fashion, the

public entertainment rooms open from this generous space. These rooms are decorated with Millard's hand-carved fireplace mantels and door surrounds and with Shutze's dramatic drapery. Each mantel has a different architectural framework: for the living room mantel, floral detailing occurs below a pediment; in the dining room, cornucopia detail the surround, which is topped with a broken pediment supported by clusters of Ionic columns.

230. Hightower House. Shutze's design here incorporates the clients' interest in Montpelier, James Madison's house in Virginia.

The only exception to the classical detailing in the Hightower house is the Gothic tracery that is subtly placed within the library's bookcase doors. Eclectic architects considered such a reference to the Gothic style appropriate in libraries through its association with learning or introversion, as in American or English colleges or European monasteries.

The house is constructed in Shutze's favorite Flemish bond, which uses alternating header and stretcher bricks, usually with dark headers. Since the Hightowers were unable to locate local masons who knew how to lay Flemish bond, Shutze volunteered to instruct the masons. He arrived on the site, rolled up his sleeves, donned a mason's apron and began laying brick.[11]

Throughout the late 1930s and 1940s, the firm's most numerous and lucrative

189

231. Southern Bell Administration Building. The scale of the building, seen here as it stood originally in Charleston, S.C., has been destroyed by later additions.

commissions involved work for the Southern Bell Telephone and Telegraph Company; over two hundred commissions were received from this one client. Some buildings were administrative offices, but the majority were "dial buildings," which housed few workers and were basically enclosures for equipment. The designs of both building types included provisions for vertical expansion, a constraint that made it especially difficult for Shutze to honor scale and proportion. Yearly, Shutze produced dozens of individualized facades, each one generally reflecting the style, materials, and climate of the local architecture. Some designs, such as the Southern Bell office in Charleston, South Carolina (1938) (*figure 231*), were exceptionally well-considered. For this structure Shutze studied the local historic architecture, particularly the work of William Jay. In the early nineteenth century Jay practiced in both Savannah and Charleston and while in Savannah produced the much admired Owens-Thomas House (1817–19), the Scarbrough house (1819), and the Telfair house (1820). For his design precedent, Shutze turned to Jay's William Mason Smith house (ca. 1820) at 26 Meeting Street in Charleston (*figure 232*), a fine example of federal or Regency architecture with its round-headed windows, Greek fret ornament, stucco walls, and a strong

232. William Mason Smith House, Charleston, S.C., of ca. 1820 by William Jay. Shutze appreciated the severe qualities of Jay's Regency designs and studied them for several buildings designed in the 1930s and 40s.

sense of fully restrained geometric simplicity.[12] Shutze used these features to transform a Charleston-style house into a contemporary public building.[13] Shutze's building sits on a rusticated base with linear coursing, which originally supported equal floors above. The entry is strong and simple with Doric columns in antis beneath a simple architrave. Originally, wood clapboard houses surrounded this structure, and although it was a public building, it was compatible in scale and rhythm with its neighbors. The building and its site were altered dramatically in 1941 and 1946, when it was enlarged both vertically and also in its depth.

Shutze produced many other interesting Southern Bell buildings because, as M. O. Saggus, a friend and colleague, observed, he "enjoyed taking some little nothing and making a gem out of it."[14] The projects represent a broad range of historical styles, from the reserved classicism of the Savannah, Georgia, administration building (*figure 233*), to the American colonial appearance of a dial office building in Bowling Green, Kentucky, designed with brick walls, slate roof, and false chimneys for American Telephone and Telegraph Company (*figure 234*).

In order to obtain the proper scale and detailing for his facades, Shutze sometimes created false windows, backed with blackened plywood if the interiors

233. *Southern Bell Administration Building. Shutze created urbanistically sympathetic buildings, such as this one in Savannah, through his close attention to scale, materials, and detailing.*

234. *Proposed dial office for American Telephone and Telegraph Company. Shutze invested even simple utilitarian buildings with humanizing details. A basic equipment building in Bowling Green, Ky., here is designed as a house with a base water table, false chimneys, and residentially scaled windows and doors.*

233

234

could not justify their existence. By 1950 new technology had removed most people from the dial offices and replaced them with delicate machinery sensitive to changes in temperature. The current taste in modern design sanctioned buildings with neither detailing nor with windows, and this image appealed to the telephone company.

Shutze might have continued to produce carefully conceived variants for projects such as these had not Southern Bell determined to cut its building expenses. Where Shutze wanted to employ Flemish bond brick patterning, Southern Bell insisted on the cheaper common bond; where Shutze specified false windows in his facades to maintain scale, Southern Bell could not agree to nonfunctioning elements. Undetailed modern architecture appealed to the pragmatic Southern Bell executives, and they began to demand it. In what one can imagine were heated dicussions, Shutze refused to design even purely functional equipment buildings without a sense of scale and detailing and, when Southern Bell threatened to find a new—one could read modern—designer, Armistead terminated his professional association with Shutze after almost fifteen years.

A second client, Piedmont Hospital, provided perhaps the conclusive evidence to Armistead that modernism was required for corporate financial success in the 1950s (*figure 235*). Piedmont Hospital came to the firm of Shutze and Armistead in part because of Shutze's association with the chief of staff, Dr. Floyd McRae, for whom an extraordinary English manor house on Habersham Road had been built. Shutze also had prior experience in hospital design for the Emory Univeristy Hospital and the maternity wing and nurse's home at Crawford Long Hospital. The directors of Piedmont Hospital wanted to move from their antiquated in-town location to the developing area at Peachtree and Collier Roads. For this location Shutze designed a master plan for a doctor's building, nurse's

235

home, and future office building expansion, and a detailed plan and elevation of
the hospital itself (*figure 236*).

His basic design is a nine-story oval mass from which project four seven-
story wings. The composition is entered through a great classical rotunda with a
Roman dome. The organization is clear, circulation is axial, and rooms and
functions are hierarchically arranged. The base and parapet of the building are
detailed in stone; the intermediate floors are brick, and the composition is capped
by a column base/elevator house. The design of a complex, almost civic building,
was the strong suit of the classicist.

One must imagine the reasons for rejection—financial concerns, or more
probably, the new attitude that a medical building should present a scientific,
modern appearance. In any case, the commission went to Armistead's newly
established firm and their solution is visible today. The realized design is high
1950s modernism with its asymmetrical plan and massive brick walls with punched
window openings.

In 1950 Shutze established his own office. He continued to share space with
the Armistead office until 1954, when the Armistead group moved from the

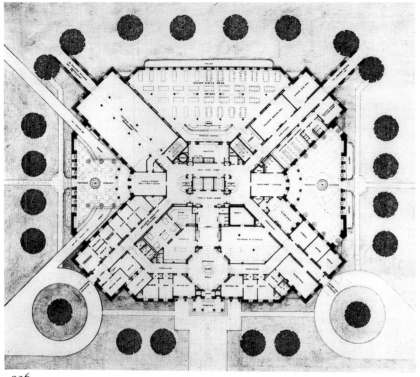

236

Candler building to a modern, air-conditioned office building they had designed. Shutze maintained an office in the Candler building—in much smaller quarters—until the year prior to his death, but his practice of architecture continued for less than a decade.

This second phase of Shutze's career coincided with his middle age; it began when he was forty-six when the association with Armistead commenced and it ran to the termination of their partnership when Shutze was sixty. In his maturity, Shutze should have realized his development as a classicist, but architectural movements and his new clientele prevented him from ever reaching the height of his abilities. For over thirty years of professional life, Shutze did not change his methods of design; his limits were imposed externally, not internally.

Shutze never put into words his confrontation with modernism; he never reflected in writing on the ways in which modernism affected his career. The evidence of his distaste for modern design and the absence of modern styling in his work indicate that he preferred not to compromise the humanistic values that he felt classical architecture brought to social life, but he accepted with great reluctance the personal consequences of his position.

237. *Daniel House, garden facade. The elaborately framed title block typifies the renderings Shutze presented to his clients.*

V
NEGLECT AND REDISCOVERY:
SHUTZE'S LAST YEARS

238. Philip Trammell Shutze in the Daniel house, 1957.

In the last three decades of his life, Shutze divided his time between architecture and his collections of porcelain, furniture, and rare books. Since he had never married, his personal life and professional interests were inextricably intertwined. The objects he collected expressed an abiding interest in eighteenth-century life; indeed, his great-niece Scotty Pannell commented that Shutze would have preferred to live in the eighteenth century.

The final phase of Shutze's professional career extended from 1950 to about 1960. The virtual termination of his architecture career at a relatively youthful seventy years stems from both the stylistic climate of the 1950s and from the office structure in which he had to function. Because he adamantly adhered to classicism, he lost commissions from large corporations whose boards of directors preferred the current image of modernism in their buildings. In this decade Shutze designed a small number of residences and institutional buildings, many of which did not progress beyond the preliminary design phase.

The change in office structure brought about by the departure of Armistead also caused him enormous practical difficulties. Shutze was accustomed to the support of a well-organized office. For twenty-five years he had designed projects and had drawn only preliminary presentation drawings. He was accustomed to the assistance of James Means, who helped develop his designs and who produced many of his working drawings. When the firm of Shutze and Armistead dissolved in 1950, Means moved to Albany, Georgia, and established a partnership with Edward Vason Jones (from 1965 to 1980 Jones was the architect in charge of renovations to the State Department and restoration of the Blue and Green Rooms in the White House, Washington, D.C.). Shutze continued to employ Means on his larger projects to help produce drawings, but his flow of work was too uncertain and of an insufficient size to maintain any permanent employees.

More than at any other period in his career, Shutze's built work indicates a predominant stylistic model—eighteenth-century American architecture. In the early years of his training Shutze had observed Neel Reid work with eighteenth-century American precedent and throughout his career he himself intermittently used various American models, but in the 1950s he looked to them almost exclusively. His interest in the creations of his own country follows a national trend of increasingly intense interest in American colonial and Georgian architecture, which began with the 1876 Centennial World's Fair in Philadelphia, and can be seen most clearly in McKim, Mead and White's residential designs. The renovation of Williamsburg, Virginia (beginning in 1927) received a great deal of attention in professional architecture magazines and Shutze visited Williamsburg at least once in the 1940s. He never returned to Europe after 1924, probably because his active professional life left him little time for travel. It would seem in keeping with his personal design method to study and employ the architecture that was at hand; by adapting newly accessible American models, he could further refine his classicist skills. Both his office library and his assembled scrapbooks provided him with a wealth of images from which to develop his own compositions in various American styles.

One of his earliest fully developed American works is the W. H. Kiser house of 1929 known as Knollwood. Shutze developed this house from his study of Chatham in Stratford County, Virginia (1765). He translated the original stucco house into a brick Georgian mass with a one-story portico that spans the curving arrival drive.

Shutze's interest in American architecture was spurred by a small commission from Mrs. Virginia Campbell Courts in 1939. The then Miss Campbell commissioned Shutze to renovate her mother's living room to accommodate a pair of Samuel McIntyre (1757–1811) mirrors, which she had recently added to her own collection of eighteenth-century American decorative arts. At the time Shutze questioned her interest in American design and expressed his own sentiment that the work was too plain for his taste. However, by 1941 he had begun to acquire eighteenth-century porcelain and American furniture for his collections. As his collections developed, so apparently did his architectural interest.

In the 1930s and 1940s Shutze designed residences that refer predominantly to southern American colonial models. The story-and-a-half house with central hallway that was popular in eighteenth-century Virginia presented an unpretentious image for residential design. Shutze employed this form in a house for his aunt Mrs. Thomas Erwin in 1934. When its original site was developed for an office building, the house was moved to Buckhead, the location of most of Shutze's important Atlanta residences, and is now the home of Catherine Maynard, Shutze's cousin. He used similar American colonial images for the William Healy and Rutherford Ellis houses, both from the late 1930s.

At the request of Harry Dwoskin, Shutze designed a modest interpretation of the Governor's Palace at Williamsburg, Virginia (*figure 239*) in 1948. The importance of the commission to Shutze derived from his lengthy professional association with the Dwoskins and their companies, first with Morris Dwoskin and then his son Harry Dwoskin, who continued his father's painting and wall finishing companies.[1] The Dwoskins worked on many of Shutze's finest projects, including the Calhoun, Rhodes, and Inman houses, the R. J. Reynolds Plantation on Sapelo Island, Georgia, as well as on The Temple, the Whitehead Memorial Room, and the Daniel house in Greenville, South Carolina.[2] Dwoskin's reputation developed from a concern for the highest quality of workmanship, and this demand for excellence may be seen in the house he commissioned.

Shutze attended meticulously to the detailing of the residence. He demanded perfection in the Flemish bond brickwork so that the coursing coordinated with the salmon colored brick door and window surrounds. To achieve greater historical accuracy, he also used wood-molded Williamsburg brick and covered the hipped roof with Buckingham slate.

He employed equally fine materials and craftsmanship on the interiors. The entry foyer included black and white marble flooring, and a Chinese Chippendale balustrade with mahogany handrail. In other public rooms, master woodcarver H. J. Millard produced exquisite overdoor detailing and mantlepieces. Dwoskin employed W. E. Browne Decorating Company to furnish draperies and rugs. Browne Decorating had as fine a reputation as Dwoskin and was employed on many of the significant residential projects in Atlanta. Shutze also depended on Browne to help in his search for antiques to add to his personal collection.

The imaginative landscape plan designed by Shutze for the Dwoskin house was not followed entirely (*figure 240*). In comparison with the sites for his other houses, the Dwoskin house site is restricted; it is a large suburban lot. Shutze originally placed a generous square entry court in front of the house as a grand eighteenth-century gesture of arrival. The garage was hidden from the public view as was the driveway leading off the entry court. But because Mrs. Dwoskin objected to the possibility of cars and trucks parking in front of her house, Shutze replaced the courtyard with a simple axial brick walk leading to the Ionic entry portico. The driveway thus lost its architectural character and became merely a typical connection of street and garage.

To the rear of the house Shutze designed a semicircular hedge to define the

239

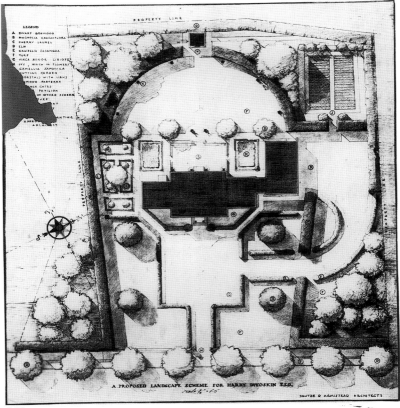

240

239. Dwoskin House,
presentation drawing
rendered by Shutze.
240. Landscape
scheme drawn by
Shutze, whose
knowledge and interest
in landscape design is
evidenced by the
variety of spaces and
garden types he
produced.

241   242

241. *Number 27
High Street, a
magazine illustration
from an office
scrapbook. Details for
Harry Dwoskin's
shops (figure 242)
were inspired by this
precedent.*

242. *The northern
portion of shops at
763 Peachtree Street
in Atlanta, remodeled
for Harry Dwoskin.*

grassed lawn and create a formal exterior space that both extended and enclosed
the house. On axis with the centerline of the house and set back from the two
defining wings of the circling hedge, he placed a small eagle-crowned garden
pavilion, which was never built.[3] He further enhanced the Dwoskin site by
defining its boundaries with a cherry laurel hedge, which, when it reached its
mature height, provided a sense of privacy seldom attained in the suburbs.

Earlier Harry Dwoskin had asked Shutze to remodel his company's offices at
763 Peachtree Street (*figure 242*; now the Atlanta Area Services for the Blind).
The existing building consisted of five shops, and the remodeling proceeded in
two stages, beginning in 1939 with the remodeling of the northern three shops
and followed later by the remaining two. To develop the design for the first three
shops Shutze selected as his precedent a 1921 magazine photograph titled "No.
27 High Street" from his architectural scrapbooks (*figure 241*). As in the later
Dwoskin residence, Shutze specified in the Dwoskin office remodeling superbly
detailed brickwork with light brick accents around the heads of windows and
doors. He personally supervised the color of the brick wall, and this aspect of
the project indicates how important the smallest of details was to the complete
design. As Shutze passed by the building each day on a city bus, it became his
custom to stop and review the mason's work from the previous day. If he noticed
too many bricks of the same tone clustered together, he would require the masons
to tear out portions of their work and rearrange the bricks. After the masons had
numerous episodes of this sort, it became their custom to applaud each city bus
that passed without dropping Shutze off to scrutinize their work.

Two additional examples of Shutze's study of eighteenth-century American

243

architecture are the M. O. Saggus house (1951) and the Charles Daniel house (1957) in Greenville, South Carolina. The quality of design and the level of workmanship demanded by Shutze indicate that his lack of commissions was not due to any decline in ability.

M. O. Saggus had joined the office in 1936, at the same time Warren Armistead did, and he remained with Shutze until 1950. When the Armistead partnership terminated, Saggus maintained his friendship with Shutze although he continued to work in Armistead's office, and at Warren Armistead's death in 1957, the firm name changed to Saggus, Williamson, Vaught, Spiker. In 1951 Saggus decided to build his own house, and when he asked Shutze to design its facade (*figure 243*), Shutze suggested that he visit the Shield house (1790) in Yorktown, Virginia; by mutual agreement Shutze adjusted the precedent to fit the needs of the Saggus family. The handsome Flemish bond brick house has a central one-story entry porch, and its main body is flanked on either side by massive chimneys.

In 1957, Shutze equaled the quality and grandeur of any of his earlier works with his Charles Daniel house in Greenville, South Carolina (*figure 246*). For both the Daniel and the earlier Dwoskin houses, Shutze used the Governor's Palace in Williamsburg as his precedent, but in the Daniel house design he blended the image of the reconstructed palace with other James River Georgian houses. The central block of the Daniel house is flanked on each side by a story-and-a-half dependency connected to the central mass. The two-story Georgian mass is capped with a cupola and widow's walk, which is connected to the upper floor by a spiral staircase. The two houses thus represent variants of classicism: the

244

Dwoskin house attempts historical fidelity to a model that transplants an English form to an English colony; the Daniel house epitomizes the earliest American variations upon their English models.

In the often repeated elements of the American Georgian style, Shutze's careful study of details separates his designs from the work of so many other architects. In this style he decided to detail his buildings entirely in molded brick. The main entrance of the Daniel house is composed of a pediment supported on two Doric columns shaped by entasis (*figure 248*). The garden entry is detailed with a pediment resting on consoles. Windows are framed with subtly curving jack arches and, to give them additional emphasis, their sills project slightly from the wall surfaces. The walls are Flemish bond, Shutze's favorite brick coursing, with raised stringcourses. The success of such detailing was assured by the client, Charles Daniel, whose construction company is still internationally recognized.

The plan differs from the anticipated Georgian arrangement of a central hall with rooms opening to either side (*figure 247*). Instead, on arrival one enters a great cube room from which rises a staircase with details by Millard. The entry axis leads into the main living room, which has delicate paneled walls with Ionic

244. *Daniel House. Herbert Millard inspects the eagle he carved for the dining room.*
245. *The eagle installed above the fireplace in the Daniel house, where Millard added a carved rose to the eagle's beak and a swag of fabric to its talons.*

pilasters and high windows which have twelve-over-nine lights. Shutze placed the principal door of the garden facade on the entry axis, but he detailed this door as a window on the interior to maintain the spatial continuity of the room and to deemphasize the circulation axis. He used the same conceptual arrangement in the Dwoskin house. Shutze designed his most exquisite architectural ornaments for the dining room. Again, he called on Millard to create the overdoors and fireplace surround (*figures 244, 245*). The fireplace wall has a two-level composition with Ionic columns, entablature, and small pediment surrounding the fireplace, and attached Corinthian columns supporting a broken pediment above. Within the pediment is a full three-dimensional eagle clutching roses in its beak and a fabric swag in its talons. As in most of his dining rooms, Shutze here used candlelight chandeliers to reinforce the room's historical character.

For the site plan, Shutze created a thoroughly American landscape, which expanded on the Georgian architecture of the house. The house is located at the crest of a hill on an axis that projects from the circling arrival drive through the house and down the hill to a set of brick pylons. The site plan is mirrored on either side of this axis with outbuildings that match one side to the other—a

246

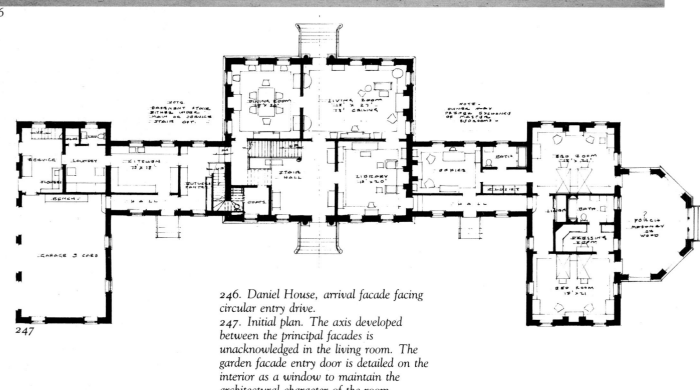

247

246. *Daniel House, arrival facade facing circular entry drive.*
247. *Initial plan. The axis developed between the principal facades is unacknowledged in the living room. The garden facade entry door is detailed on the interior as a window to maintain the architectural character of the room.*
248. *Garden facade.*

249. Citizens and Southern National Bank, East Point. Shutze renovated two buildings to create this new bank.

greenhouse on one side, a pool house on the other—and formal walled gardens on both sides. Close to the house Shutze placed geometrical massings of boxwood and azaleas symmetrically about the axis. The formality of the plantings disappears gradually, as the distance from the central axis increases until unaltered nature reimposes itself. With its walled gardens and dependencies, the site gives the distinct impression of an earlier time in American history, when the house and its immediately surrounding landscape would have attempted to impose a symbolic order on the wilderness.

The quality of the Daniel house places Shutze on a level equal with the somewhat earlier neo-Georgian architect William Lawrence Bottomley (1883–1951). The major portion of Bottomley's Georgian work is in Richmond, Virginia, and the surrounding countryside. The two architects shared an interest in creating historically accurate exteriors, but where Bottomley carried this concern inside, Shutze allowed himself greater freedom of expression. Shutze's interiors are not historic reconstructions, but complex mixtures of attitudes—a powerful classical interior space is often paired with a delicately detailed room, as in the living and dining rooms of the Daniel house.

In the few nonresidential commissions that Shutze received in the final years

250

251

of his practice, he also employed eighteenth-century American architecture as his source of design inspiration. The Citizens and Southern National Bank (for whom he had designed the Roman and mannerist detailed main banking room [1929–31]) frequently commissioned Shutze to design branch banks, and in the 1950s he received three such projects from them. This is the only major corporate work produced by Shutze in this period and it was available because the client refused to accept modern styling for their architectural image.

The banks, produced for the small Georgia towns of East Point, Thomaston, and Newnan, share similarities in materials and general character (*figures 249–251*). Shutze selected early eighteenth-century American architecture as the stylistic basis for these designs, and he emulated not only the typical materials of Flemish bond brickwork, sparkling white trim, and slate roofs, but also the use of residential elements to soften public architecture—a procedure characteristic of America's early efforts at developing a public architecture. The East Point bank (1953) owes its general outline to the two existing buildings that Shutze remodeled to accommodate the new banking function. Shutze enhanced the resulting irregular massing with Williamsburg brick, deep cornice moldings, and a canopied entry door. The scale and outline are reminiscent of eighteenth-

250. Citizens and Southern National Bank, Thomaston. This freestanding building is appropriately scaled for its small-town context.

251. Citizens and Southern National Bank, Newnan. Shutze employed the same plan as in the Thomaston bank, but achieved variety in the facade details appropriate to this more urban context.

252. *Goddard Chapel, Grady Memorial Hospital. The room's classical detailing contrasts with its context of a modern hospital.*
253. *Detail of the chapel.*

252

century townhouses in Philadelphia. The Newnan (1957) and Thomaston banks (1957) were apparently designed together, and like the East Point bank, each expresses an unpretentious character appropriate to their locations in small town centers. Each has a single-gable roofed mass with its narrow face to the street, and each plan is virtually identical. Shutze detailed the Thomaston bank with large bow windows in the spirit of a commercial building in Williamsburg, but of a larger scale. The Newnan bank is more reserved with a plainly detailed raking and horizontal cornices and double-hung windows with sixteen-over-sixteen lights on the first floor. Its major difference is an adaptation to a sloping site. The two banks demonstrate Shutze's development of a historical model and the variations he could achieve in his own detailing.

Both Shutze's use of American models and his disinterest in modernism are evident in his design for the Goddard Chapel (*figure 252*; dedicated 1956). The chapel is located deep within the interior of Grady Memorial Hospital (1954–58), designed with a modern plan and detailing by the Atlanta architectural and engineering firm of Robert and Company. The chapel commission forced Shutze to work within a modern context, but he made no attempt to relate his design

254

255

256

to the massive structure that contained it. Instead, he allowed the religious nature of his program to direct his style selection to what was termed an American adaptation of the Queen Anne style. The small room has a comfortable, familiar appearance when it is discovered within the hospital's antiseptic labyrinth of corridors and rooms. The chapel's walls are white wood paneling decorated by elaborately swagged curtains. The room is furnished with traditional pews and pulpit, and the altar end is decorated with the ten commandments on tablets. The success of the space as a foil to the pure functional quality of the remainder of the building must have assured Shutze of the continuing need for classical architecture in the context of a highly scientific modern world.

After 1960 Shutze closed his practice, but he maintained an office in the Candler building, principally to house his vast office library. In 1968, however, he became involved in one last design project for the Atlanta Historical Society, then located in the Willis Jones house. That house was a Neel Reid design that had been renamed McElreath Hall in honor of the society's founder Walter McElreath. By the late 1960s the society had outgrown the Jones house, and in 1965 it acquired Swan house and its twenty-three acre site. Mrs. Edward Inman first offered to sell her house to the state of Georgia as a new governor's mansion and, when that offer was declined, she offered it to the Atlanta Historical Society. In the same year, funds from the Walter McElreath Foundation became available for the society's use and after lengthy discussions, the society purchased the property.[4] In the summer of 1967, the society moved into its new quarters, and the Anglo-Italian baroque classicist masterpiece that Shutze had designed forty years earlier became the repository of Atlanta's social history.

The new use for the property required some architectural adjustments, most significantly, the installation of security gates at the driveway entrance to Swan house on Andrews Drive. Shutze had proposed gates in his original scheme, but at the time Mrs. Inman found no need for an imposing entry. In 1968 he reworked his original scheme and presented it to the society for their consideration (*figures 254, 255*). Using as his model the gates at the Villa Borghese in Rome, Shutze designed a wrought iron fence between twin rusticated guard houses; he adjusted the model by placing nesting swans above each small building.[5] This dramatic design would have been an appropriate entry for his baroque villa, but the society decided that it was too expensive and selected another architect to supply a

254. Inman House gates, study. Shutze considered this scheme for gates, on Andrews Drive, which were on axis with the garden facade of the house. 255. The final proposal for entry gates to the house, of 1968, followed the general scheme for the gates for the Villa Borghese in Rome, modified by a pair of nesting swans. "Swan House" was Mrs. Inman's name for her home and the current title given the house. 256. The house is now occupied by the Atlanta Historical Society. Shutze's proposed expansion (unbuilt) of 1968 called for a suite of rooms to accommodate new functional requirements of that institution.

257. Shutze House, elevation. In his sixties, Shutze designed several residential schemes for himself, such as this one of 1955. The designs all included a private office and drafting room.

modest gate in keeping with the Italian character of the garden facade of the Swan house.

Anticipating the society's growth, Shutze in the same year also proposed a design that he described as a future addition, a wing, or separate building to Swan house. It would accommodate a grand ballroom, a dining room, state functions, and a museum (*figure 256*).[6] This scheme, which exists only as an interior elevation, consists of three interconnecting elements: a central double-cube room flanked on either side by single-cube rooms.[7] On the rendering Shutze listed as his "general inspiration" English and Italian sources congruent with the mixed character of the main house: the double-cube and single-cube rooms at Wilton house, Wiltshire; Wentworth Castle, Yorkshire; and the Palazzo Colonna, Rome. Although his scheme was not accepted, the drawing indicates Shutze's undiminished classicist imagination and rendering skills.

After closing his architecture office, Shutze devoted most of his time to his decorative arts collections. As early as his student days in Rome, he had begun to collect architecture books that were important to his practice, but in the 1940s he also began to collect porcelain and furniture systematically. As befits a classicist

258. Philip Shutze in his apartment surrounded by his collections of porcelain, books, and furniture. The false walls he designed for additional storage were located after his death to the second floor of the Atlanta Historical Society as a part of a permanent display of his collections.

architect, his interests were eclectic, and he amassed a sizable collection of approximately 700 ceramic pieces, including Chinese export and Meissen. His furniture collection included approximately 100 pieces, principally American, with multiple examples of all the major forms. Shutze made his last purchase in 1980 at the age of ninety, a Chinese export group of Tyrolean dancers (1750–60), which he had sought for years to obtain.

He had intended to build a house for himself and his collections of books, porcelain, and furniture, but he never did (*figure 257*). Between 1951 and 1955 he designed two separate but related residential schemes. In plan the houses were traditional Georgian layouts with central hallways; each design included a distinct office area with a drafting room and a private office. In elevation the designs were one-and-a-half-story brick with slate gambrel roofs. As was his custom, he developed numerous interior details in small pencil sketches. In the only rendered elevation of his house design, Shutze incorporated a slightly projecting gable over the entry door, which is topped with a decorative thistle and is inscribed with the Latin phrase *ad alba vigilis*.

Shutze lived with his sister Faye Shutze Cates and her family for thirty-two

259. *Shutze's living room in his apartment, for which he made dozens of sketches of possible arrangements of furniture and porcelain.*

years until they sold their property in 1958. He then moved into his own apartment on Peachtree Road; his sister and her husband had an apartment in the same building. Shutze's two-bedroom apartment was far too small for his collections; he used any surface—even the oven of his stove and a second bathtub—and all unused floor space to store his porcelain (*figures 258–260*). He kept much of his furniture at the Browne Decorating Company, and some pieces he never uncrated. His collections ultimately found a worthy home with his bequest to the Atlanta Historical Society of all his personal belongings. His porcelain and furniture collections are displayed on the second floor of Swan house in the four bedrooms. One room has been altered to resemble Shutze's living room; it includes a paneled wall and tiled fireplace, which he added to his own apartment. His office library, drawings, and architectural memorabilia are housed in the McElreath Hall Research Library on the Swan house grounds.

In addition to collecting, Shutze's favorite pastimes were painting and camellia horticulture. He painted in oil and watercolor, and he created many decorative objects for his family. He was never satisfied with the results of his painting, and he destroyed all of them. Most of Shutze's interests—architecture, furniture, porcelain—relate to the eighteenth century. His interest in camellias was historically consistent. They were first brought to England from China in 1677, and by the end of the eighteenth century they were grown in America. Camellias were especially popular in Charleston, Savannah, and Mobile. They appealed to Shutze because he preferred to design green gardens, a taste he developed from his admiration of northern Italian villas. By his own account he

260. *A large print of a view of Rome from the Janiculum, on which the American Academy in Rome is located, hung in Shutze's living room.*

was one of the first to grow camellias in a protected greenhouse rather than subject them to the fickle winter weather of Atlanta. He introduced many of his clients to camellia horticulture through the gardens he incorporated into their site plans. He had created an Oriental-style camellia house on May Goodrum's estate, and for other clients he included camellias in the landscaping. The evidence of these gardens has for the most part disappeared because the north Georgia climate has proved to be unsuitable for camellias. His own greenhouse and that of May Goodrum were destroyed by later owners.[8]

Shutze designed an extensive garden for his brother-in-law Alvin Cates, and he included a large greenhouse for himself. Both men were avid gardeners, but Shutze was uninterested in Cates's flower and vegetable gardens. He preferred to work in his heated greenhouse, where he ultimately grew over 200 varieties of camellias. He displayed his blooms at camellia shows (*figure 261*), and around 1935 he received a medal from the Garden Club of America for one of them. He even designed temporary architectural backdrops for the annual Atlanta Camellia Show at the Atlanta Biltmore Hotel. One ornate classical backdrop included a wall surface with a niche that surrounded half a column draped in silver fabric. A laurel wreath topped the column and this entire arrangement served as the display pedestal for prize-winning blooms (*figure 262*). In other years he created a classical colonnade, an oriental set (*figure 263*) and a Japanese tea house.

Shutze maintained his interest in architecture, but the disparity between the sanctioned styles of the 1950s to 1970s and his own sense of aesthetics caused him great distress. He abhorred modernism and steadfastly believed it would prove

261

262

261. *Shutze's prize-winning camellias presented in his cut-out paper doves.*

262. *Shutze designed the frontispiece for the Atlanta Camellia Show held at the Biltmore Hotel in 1949.*

no more than temporarily intriguing to architects and clients alike. In an unpublished article titled "The Decorative Arts," Shutze expressed his sentiments about the modern style in all the arts:

> It is the duty of the present generation to preserve what we have of value for the level of taste has sunk to an unprecedented state and our productions are blue denim and ersatz.
>
> Architecture, the mistress of the fine arts has given away to engineering. Painting is comparatively non-existent and sculpture contrived amorphous masses. An unruly blob of harsh colour is just as satisfying to the painter of today as a really good painting and certainly much less trouble.
>
> Charlatanism is rife![9]

On 8 January 1979 the cover story of *Time* magazine featured Robert Hughes's article on postmodernism and the often reported death of modernism. In the opening paragraph Hughes wrote: "The 1970s were the decade in which modernism died. Its Boot Hill turned out to be the U.S., in whose hospitable soil the dreams of the pioneers of modern art and architecture lie buried, toes to the rising sun. Once they hoped the world would be made whole by new paintings and new buildings. It was not, and there is no avant-garde any more; the very phrase has been scrapped, becoming one of the historical curiosities of criticism."[10]

Whether this was Shutze's first exposure to the concept of postmodernism is unclear, but he received the news with great enthusiasm. He wrote to at least three friends—Allyn Cox, Henry Hope Reed, and Jack Spalding—to recommend the article which "dumps the whole modern movement in architecture on the trash pile."[11] His enthusiasm for the content of the article drove him to request Jack Spalding, the retired editor of the *Atlanta Journal*, to reprint the entire eight

pages in the newspaper. Shutze wrote to Spalding: "How fine it would be if the paper could reprint this article to inform the public how they are being led like sheep by an illiterate bunch of architect engineers to design the type of thing that is ruining our city with amorphous masses of steel and glass."[12]

Although generations of Atlanta architects had recognized his abilities, it was not until the advent of postmodernism and its reawakened interest in classicism that Shutze received some degree of national attention. Henry Hope Reed, founder of Classical America and one of the earliest critics of modernism, brought national attention to Shutze with an exhibition of his work at Columbia University in 1979. Two years earlier, Reed had used his work as the focus for *Classical America IV*, naming him "America's Greatest Living Classical Architect." In the Introduction to this issue, William A. Coles wrote, "We are especially pleased to join with the Atlanta Historical Society in documenting and paying homage to the remarkable work of Philip Shutze. That so fine an architect should be so little known outside Georgia testifies to the blindness of modernism. Not only does it expunge history from its own creation; it also edits history to delete silently what it cannot appreciate."[13] These two events, the exhibition and the article, brought Shutze more national exposure than he had received during his entire career.

Shutze's first local recognition came in 1951, when he was elected a fellow in the American Institute of Architects without ever actively participating in the organization. Changing attitudes toward modernism caused many architects to reassess Shutze's architectural contributions to the city, and in 1974 the Georgia Chapter of the AIA awarded him their bronze medal for achievement in design.

Shutze's association with Swan house had always been extremely important to him, and when it became the headquarters for the Atlanta Historical Society in 1967 he received even further recognition. In 1975, the society organized the first exhibition of his full career in architecture. In 1977, he allowed his porcelain collection to be displayed publicly for the first time. Each event drew large appreciative audiences. Shutze received additional recognition in his last years. In 1978 he was recognized by the Governor's Awards for the Arts, and in 1979 he received a Career Award of Excellence from the Atlanta Urban Design Commission and a Doctorate of Humane Letters from Emory University.

Although his alma mater, Georgia Tech, had taken little advantage of his abilities through the years—he never designed a campus building, never taught after the early 1920s, and seldom served as a critic—the architecture students of the early 1980s were intrigued with his work.[14] The student chapter of the AIA initiated an annual recognition designated the "Philip Trammell Shutze Distinguished Alumni Award" and commissioned the nationally recognized sculptor (and fellow Tech alumnus) Julian Harris to design an appropriate medal. Shutze received the award during his final period of hospitalization in 1982. So moved by the long overdue recognition, he wore the beribboned medal until his death on 17 October 1982.

In his personal life Shutze remained quite close to his family, and his personality epitomized the old eccentric southern bachelor. He had many acquaintances, but few close friends; his cousin Catherine Maynard and his associate James Means were his most frequent visitors. He received the admiration of many of his clients, and his active social life gave him no time to become reclusive.

His strongest and most constant friend was Allyn Cox, his fellow Academy student and professional colleague, who shared with Shutze for sixty-six years dreams of a noble career and its accompanying fame. In the early years, Shutze helped his friend enormously, including him in the work on the Calhoun house and, in the bleak 1930s, the Goodrum house. Cox later received much national recognition for his work in the United States House of Representatives, the Capitol Rotunda, and other projects. Shutze visited Cox and his wife in New York and they exchanged Christmas presents and corresponded regularly. Shutze received his last letter from Cox the year they both died; that letter closes with the memory of what must have sustained each man's creativity: "I think of you often, and the old days in Rome."[15]

APPENDIX I

Books on English and Italian Architecture and Landscape Architecture
in the office library of Philip Trammell Shutze

At his death Shutze's office and personal libraries were willed to the Atlanta Historical Society. Few libraries of twentieth century American classical architects exist intact, and therefore the composition of his collection is significant not only as a personal artifact, but also as a general indication of the design sources employed by his contemporaries. In total, his collection contains 1756 items. The following bibliography covers English and Italian architecture and landscape architecture. A complete bibliography is available at McElreath Hall at the Atlanta Historical Society.

Acton, Harold. *Great Houses of Italy: the Tuscan Villas.* With photos by Alexander Zielcke. New York: Viking Press, 1973.

Adam, Robert. *Ruins of the Palace of the Emperor Diocletian at Spalatro in Dalmatia.* London: The Author, 1764.

Adam, Robert. *The Architecture, Decoration, and Furniture of Robert and James Adam.* London: B.T. Batsford, 1880.

Adam, Robert. *The Works in Architecture of Robert and James Adam, Esquires.* London: Peter Elmsly, 1778; reprinted by E. Thezard Filo, Dourdan, 1900. 2 vols.

American Architect: Architectural Details of Northern Italy. 1914–1916.

Architectural Reprint: Misc. plates by Belcher & Macartney, James Biggs and Batty Langley, [n.d.].

Architecture of Sir Roger Pratt, Charles II's Commissioner for the Rebuilding of London after the Great Fire. Oxford: John Johnson for the Author, 1928.

Barozzi, Giacomo. *The Five Orders of Architecture, by Giacomo Barozzi of Vignola.* Norwood, Me.: Norwood Press, Berwick & Smith, 1889.

Belcher, John. *Later Renaissance Architecture in England.* London: B.T. Batsford: New York: Charles Scribner's Sons, 1901. 2 vols.

Beunat, Joseph. *Empire Style Designs and Ornaments.* New York: Dover, 1974.

Beveridge, Thomas J. *English Renaissance Woodwork, 1660–1730.* New York: Architectural Book Publishing Co., Paul Wenzel L & Maurice Krakow; London: B.T. Batsford, 1921.

Bolton, Arthur T. *The Architecture of Robert & James Adam, 1758–1794.* London: Country Life, George Newnes; New York: Charles Scribner's Sons, 1922.

Bonham-Carter, Victor. *The English Village.* Harmondsworth, Middlesex: Penguin Books, 1952.

Borgatti, Mariano. *Castel Sant'Angelo in Rome.* Rome: La Liberia dello Stato, [n.d.].

Braun, Hugh. *The Story of the English House.* London: B.T. Batsford, 1940.

Brunelli, Bruno. *Ville del Brenta e Degli Euganei.* Milano: Fratelli Treves, 1931–1939.

Campbell, Colin. *Vitruvius Britannicus; or, the British Architect.* London: The Author, 1725. 3 vols.

Canina, Luigi. *Gli Edifizj di Roma Antica, Cogniti per Alcune Reliquie, Descritti e Dimostrati nell'intera Loro Architettura.* Roma: Dai Tipi, 1848; G.A. Bertinelli, 1851,1856. 6 vols.

Chievrici, Gino. *La Reggia di Caserta.* Roma: La Libreria dello Stato, 1937.

Cicognara, L. *Le Fabbriche e i Monumenti Cospicui di Venezia.* Venezia: Giuseppe Antonelli et Luciano Basadonna, 1858. 2 vols.

Clunn, Harold P. *The Face of London.* New & rev. ed. London: Spring Books, 1951.

Coats, Peter. *Great Gardens of Britain.* New York: Putnam, 1967.

Coats, Peter. *The Gardens of Buckingham Palace*. London: Michael Joseph, 1978.

Colasanti, Arduino. *Volte e Soffitti Italiane*. Milano: Casa Editrice d'Arte, Bestetti & Tumminelli, 1915.

Complete Work of Raphael. New York: Reynal & Co., in association with William Morrow, 1969.

Darly, Matthias. *The Ornamental Architect, or Young Artists Instructor, Consisting of the Five Orders, drawn by Aliquot, parts with their Embellishments, etc., Elegantly Engraved on [102] folio-Plates by Various Masters*. London: The Author, 1770?

Davie, W. Galsworthy. *Old Cottages and Farmhouses in Kent and Sussex*. London: B.T.Batsford, 1900.

Davie, W. Galsworthy. *Old Cottages and Farmhouses in Surrey*. London: B.T. Batsford, 1908.

Davis, Terence. *The Architecture of John Nash*. London: Studio, 1960.

Dening, C.F.W. *The Eighteenth-Century Architecture of Bristol*. Bristol: J.W. Arrowsmith, 1923.

Disegni di Vari Altari e Cappelle nelle Chiese di Roma con le Loro Facciate Franchi Piante e Misure de piu Celebri Architetti. Rome: Gio. Giacomo de Rossi, [n.d.].

Eberlein, Harold Donaldson. *Details of the Architecture of Tuscany*. New York: William Helburn, 1923.

Eberlein, Harold Donaldson. *Villas of Florence and Tuscany*. Philadelphia: J.B. Lippincott; New York: Architectural Record, 1922.

English Mediaeval Foliage. [n.d.].

Espouy, Hector d'. *Fragment d'Architecture Antique d'apres les Releves & Restaurations des Anciens Pensionnaires d'Academie de France a Rome*. Paris: Charles Schmid, Editeur, 1905. 2 vols.

Espouy, Hector d'. *Fragments from Greek and Roman Architecture: the Classical American Edition of Hector d'Espouy's Plates*. Introductory notes by John Blatteau and Christiane Sears. New York: Norton, 1981.

Espouy, Hector d'. *Fragments d'Architecture du Moyen Age et de la Renaissance & Restaurations des Anciens Pensionnaires d'Academie de France a Rome*. Paris: Massin et Cie, Editeurs, 1925. 2 vols.

Esquie, Pierre. *The Five Orders of Architecture, the Casting of Shadows and the First Principles of Construction, Based on the System of Vignola*. New York: William Helburn, [n.d.].

Farrar, et al. *Westminster Abbey and the Cathedrals of England*. Philadelphia: John C. Winston, 1895.

Fasolo, Giulio. *Le Ville del Vicentino*. Vicenza: Arti Grafiche delle Venezie, 1929.

Ferrari, Giulio. *Il Ferro, nell'arte Italiana, Riproduzioni in Gran Parte inedite di 169 Soggetti del Medioevo del Rinascimento, del periodo Barocco e Neo-Classico*. Milano: Ulrico Hoepli, Libraio della Real Casa, 1910.

Ferrari, Giulio. *Il Legno, nell'Arte Italiana, Riproduizioni in parte inedite di saggi dal Periodo Romanico al Neo-Classico*. Milano: Ulrico Hoepli, Librario della Real Casa, 1910.

Ferrari, Giulio. *La Tomba, nell'Arte Italiana dal Periodo Preromano all'Adierno*. Milano: Ulrico Hoepli, Librario della Real Casa, 1916.

Ferrari, Giulio. *Lo Stucco, nell'Arte Italiana, Riproduzioni in Parte inedite di Saggi dal Periodo Etrusco al Neo-Classico*. Milano: Ulrico Hoepli, Librario della Real Casa, 1910.

Field, Horace. *English Domestic Architecture of the XVII and XVIII Centuries*. London: George Bell & Sons, 1905.

Garner, Thomas. *The Domestic Architecture of England during the Tudor Period*. London: B.T. Batsford, 1911. 3 vols.

Georgian Society. *Records of Eighteenth-Century Domestic Architecture and Decoration in Dublin*. Dublin: Dublin University Press, 1909. 5 vols.

Gibbs, James. *A Book of Architecture, Containing Designs of Buildings and Ornaments*. London: 1728.

Gnoli, D. *Have Roma*. Roma: Walter Modes, 1909.

Gotch, J. Alfred. *Early Renaissance Architecture in England, a Historical & Descriptive Account of the Tudor, Elizabethan, & Jacobean Periods, 1500–1625*. 2nd ed. rev. London: B.T. Batsford, 1904.

Gotch, J. Alfred. *The English Home, from Charles I to George IV, its Architecture, Decoration, and Garden Design*. London: B.T. Batsford, 1919, 1918. 2 vols.

Great Houses of Italy by the Editors of Realites. Text under the direction of Claude Fregnac. New York: Putnam, 1968.

Green, Mowbray A. *The Eighteenth Century Architecture of Bath*. Bath: George Gregory, 1904.

Grinling Gibbons and His Compeers. London: J. Tiranti, 1914.

Gromort, G. *Choix d'Elements Empruntes a l'Architecture Classique*. 2nd ed. Paris: Aug. Vincent, 1907.

Grosso, Orlando. *Portali e Palazzi di Genova*. Milano: Bestetti & Tumminelli, [n.d.].

Gusman, Pierre. *L'Art Decoratif de Rome, de la fin de la Republique au IV siecle*. Paris: Librairie Centrale d'Art et Architecture; Ancienne Maison Morel, Ch. Eggimann, 1914.

Hadas, Moses. *Imperial Rome, by Moses Hadas and the Editors of Time-Life Books*. New York: Time, Inc., 1965.

Hall, S.C. *The Baronial Halls and Ancient Picturesque Edifices of England*. London: Willis & Sotheran, 1858. 2 vols.

Harris, John. *A Garden Alphabet*. London: Octopus Books in Association with Edgeworth Press, 1979.

Hielscher, Kurt. *Picturesque Italy, Architecture and Landscape*. New York: Brentano's; [Berlin, Ernst Wasmuth], 1925.

Holme, Charles. *The Gardens of England in the Northern Counties*. London: The Studio, 1911.

Hooker, Marion O. *Farmhouses and Small Provincial Buildings in Southern Italy*. New York: Architectural Book Publishing Co., Paul Wenzel & Maurice Krakow, 1925.

Iannoni, M. Giovanni. *Saggi di Architettura e Decorazione Italiana; Secola XV. XVI; Graffiti e Chiaroscura Esistenti nell'Esterno delle Case*. Rome: Enrico Massari, [n.d.].

Ison, Walter. *The Georgian Buildings of Bath, from 1700 to 1830*. New York: Charles Scribner's Sons, 1948.

Jones, Inigo. *The Designs of Inigo Jones, Consisting of Plans and Elevations for Publick and Private Buildings*. London: William Kent, 1727. 2 vols.

Jones, Owen. *The Grammar of Ornament*. London: Day & Son, 1856.

Jourdain, M. *English Decorative Plasterwork of the Renaissance*. New York: Charles Scribner's Sons; London: B.T. Batsford, 1926.

Jourdain, M. *English Interiors in Smaller Houses, from the Restoration to the Regency, 1660–1830*. New York: Charles Scribner's Sons; London: B.T. Batsford, 1923.

Jourdain, Margaret. *The Work of William Kent, Artist, Painter, Designer and Landscape Gardener*. London: Country Life; New York: Charles Scribner's Sons, 1948.

Knight, Henry Gally. *The Ecclesiastical Architecture of Italy, from the Time of Constantine to the Fifteenth Century*. London: Henry Bohn, 1843. 2 vols.

Kraus, Theodor. *Pompeii and Herculaneum: the Living Cities of the Dead*. New York: H.N. Abrams, 1975.

Langley, Batty. *Ancient Architecture, Restored & Improved, by a Great Variety of Grand and useful Designs, Entirely New in the Gothick Mode, for the ornamenting of Buildings & Gardens*. London: B. & T. Langley, 1742.

Latham, Charles. *In English Homes; the Internal Character, Furniture & Adornments of Some of the Most Notable Houses of England*. London: Country Life, George Newnes; New York, Charles Scribner's Sons, 1904. 3 vols.

Le Blond, Mrs. Aubrey. *The Old Gardens of Italy, How to Visit Them*. London: John Lane, 1912.

Lees-Milne, James. *The Age of Adam*. London: B.T. Batsford, 1947.

Letarouilly, Paul. *Edifices de Rome Moderne, ou Recueil des Palais, Maisons, Eglises, Couvents et autre Monuments Publics et Particuliers les plus Remarquables de la Ville de Rome*. Paris: A. Morel et Cie, Editeurs [1840], 1868, 1874.

Letarouilly, Paul. *Edifices de Rome Moderne, ou Recueil des Palais, Maisons, Eglises, Couvents, et autre Monuments Publics et Particuliers les plus Remarquables de la Ville de Rome*. Leige: D. Avanzo & Cie, 1853. 3 vols.

Letarouilly, Paul. *Edifices de Rome Moderne*. Misc. plates, not in order. No title page. Bound in 1 vol.

Letarouilly, Paul. *Edifices de Rome Moderne, ou Recueil des Palais, Maisons, Eglises, Couvents et autres Monuments Publics et Particuliers les plus Remarquables de la Ville de Rome*. Paris: Ve A. Morel & Cie, 1868.

Letarouilly, Paul. *Edifices de Rome Moderne, ou Recueil des Palais, Maisons, Eglises, Couvents, et autre Monuments Publics et Particuliers les plus Remarquables de la Ville de Rome*. Bruxelles: Bruylant-Christophe, 1866.

Lloyd, Nathaniel. *A History of the English House, From Primitive Times to the Victorian Period*. New ed. London: Architectural Press, 1948.

Loukomski, G.K. *L'Ouvre d'Andrea Palladio: Les Villas des Doges de Venise*. Paris: Albert Morance, [n.d.]. 2 vols.

Loukomski, George. *Charles Cameron (1740–1812): an Illustrated Monograph on his Life and Work in Russia, Particularly at Tsarkoe, Selo and Pavlovsk*. London: Nicholson & Watson, Commodore Press, 1943.

Lowell, Guy. *More Small Italian Villas and Farmhouses*. New York: Architectural Book Publishing Co., 1920.

Lowell, Guy. *Smaller Italian Villas and Farmhouses*. New York: Architectural Book Publishing Co., Paul Wenzel & Maurice Krakow, 1916.

Macartney, Mervyn E. *Standard Examples of Architectural Details*. New York: Architectural Book Publishing Co., 1913.

Magni, Giulo. *Il Barocco a Roma, nell'Architettura e nella

Scultura Decorativa. Torino: C. Crudo, 1911–1913. 3 vols.

Masson, Georgina. *Italian Gardens*. New York: Abrams, 1961.

Mau, August. *Pompeii, its Life and Art*. New York: Macmillan, 1899.

Mazzotti, Guiseppe. *Ville Venete*. New ed. Rome: Carlo Bestetti, Edizioni d'Art, 1963.

Midana, Arturo. *L'Arte del Legno in Piemonte nel sei e nel Settecento, Mobili Decorazioni Barocchi e Rococo*. Torino: Itala Aro, [n.d.].

Misciattelli, Piero. *La Libreria Piccolomini, nel Duomo di Siena*. Siena: Guintini-Bentivoglio, 1922.

Monuments Antiques, Releves et Restaures par les Architectes Pensionnaires de l'Academie de France a Rome. Paris: Ch. Massin, Editeur, [n.d.] 4 vols.

Nash, Joseph. *Mansions of England in the Olden Time, Facades and Interiors in English Gothic and Renaissance*. New York: Bruno Hessling, 190-?

Nicholson, Peter. *The Carpenter and Joiner's Assistant, Containing Rules for Making All Kinds of Joints and Various Methods of Hinging them Together*. London: Printed for I. & J. Taylor at the Architectural Library, 1797.

Ornamenti Greci. 1873?–1875. 31 plates bear titles: Ornamenti Greci, Romani, Architettura Greca, Ornato romano, or no title. Last 12 plates: Pianta e prospetto: collezione ornati del Palazzo de Villa Madama. Rome: Calcographic, 1873–1875.

Pain, William. *The Practical Builder; or Workman's General Assistant*. London: Printed for I. & J. Taylor at the Architectural Library, 1787.

Palast-architektur von Ober-Italien und Toscana. Berlin: Ernst Wasmuth, 1903–1922. 6 vols.

Palladio, Andrea. *The Architecture of A. Palladio; in Four Books Containing a Short Treatise of the Five Orders and the Most Necessary Observations Concerning All Sorts of Buildings*. 2nd ed. London: John Darby, 1721.

Palladio, Andrea. *The Four Books of Architecture*, With a New Introduction by Adolf K. Placzek. New York: Dover Publications, 1965.

Palladio, Andrea. *I Quattro Libri dell'Architettura*. Venezia: Bartolomeo Carampello, 1601.

Percier, C. *Romische Villen und Parkanlagen, nach Maisons de Plaisance de Rome et de ses Environs*. Berlin: Bruno Hessling, [n.d.].

Pergolesi, Michel Angelo. *Classical Ornament of the Eight-eenth Century, Designed & Engraved by Michel Angelo Pergolesi*. New York: Dover Publications, 1970.

Pevsner, Nikolaus. *The Buildings of England, Nottinghamshire*. Harmondsworth, Middlesex: Penguin Books, 1951.

Phillips, E. March. *The Gardens of Italy*. London: Country Life & D. George Newnes; New York: Charles Scribner's Sons, 1919.

Ponti, Maria Pasolini. *Il Giardino Italiano*. Roma: Ermanno Loscher (W. Regenberg), 1915.

Practical Exemplar of Architecture. 2nd ed. London: The Architectural Press, 1927. 7 vols.

Price, Francis. *The British Carpenter: or, a Treatise on Carpentry*. 5th ed. London: H. Baldwin, 1765.

Pugin, Augustus. *Specimens of Gothic Architecture, Selected from Various Ancient Edifices in England*. 3rd ed. London: Nattali & Bond, 1821,1822. 2 vols.

Ramsey, Stanley C. *Small Houses of the Late Georgian Period, 1750–1820*. London: Technical Journals, 1919.

Ramsey, Stanley C. *Small Houses of the Late Georgian Period, 1750–1820*. New York: William Helburn; London: Architectural Press, 1923.

Reilly, Paul. *An Introduction to Regency Architecture*. New York: Pellegrini & Cudahy, 1948.

Richardson, A.E. *London Houses from 1660 to 1820*. London: B.T. Batsford, 1911.

Richardson, A.E. *The Smaller English House of the Later Renaissance, 1660–1830*. New York: William Helburn; London: B.T. Batsford, 1925.

Richardson, George. *A Book of Ceilings, in the Stile of the Antique Grotesque*. London: The Author, 1774.

Roop, Guy. *Villas & Palaces of Andrea Palladio, 1508–1580*. Milano: Francisco Ghezzi, 1968.

Rosenberg, Louis Conrad. *Cottages, Farmhouses and Other Minor Buildings of the 16th, 17th, and 18th Centuries*. New York: Architectural Book Publishing Co., Paul Wenzel and Maurice Krakow, 1923.

Rosenberg, Louis Conrad. *The Davanzati Palace, Florence, Italy, a Restored Palace of the Fourteenth Century*. New York: Architectural Book Publishing Co., Paul Wenzel & Maurice Krakow, 1922.

Ross, Janet. *Florentine Villas*. London: J.M.Dent, New York: Dutton, 1901.

Royal Pavilion at Brighton. 1972.

Rubens, Peter Paul. *Palazzi antichi di Genova. Palazzi Moderni di Genova.* With an introd. essay by Alan A. Tait. New York: Blom, 1968. 2 vols in 1.

Sadlier, Thomas U. *Georgian Mansions in Ireland, with some Account of the Evolution of Georgian Architecture and Decoration.* Dublin: Dublin University Press, 1915.

Salmon, William. *Palladio Londinensis: or, the London Art of Building.* London: Printed for S. Birt, etc., 1752.

Scherer, Margaret R. *Marvels of Ancient Rome.* New York: Phaidon Press for the Metropolitan Museum of Art, 1956.

Shepard, J.C. *Italian Gardens of the Renaissance.* New York: Charles Scribner's Sons, 1925.

Small, Tunstall. *Houses of the Wren and Early Georgian Periods.* London: Architectural Press; New York: William Helburn, 1928.

Small, Turnstall. *Architectural Turned Woodwork of the 16th, 17th & 18th Centuries, a Portfolio of Full-Size Details.* London: Architectural Press; New York: William Helburn, [n.d.].

Small, Turnstall. *Mouldings of the Wren and Georgian Periods, a Portfolio of Full-size Sections.* London: Architectural Press; New York: William Helburn, [n.d.].

Spampani, Gio Battista. *I Cinque Ordini di Architettura Civile di Giacomo Barozzi da Vignola.* Seconda Edizione Romana. Roma: Giuseppe Bianchi, 1861.

Stegmann, Carl von. *The Architecture of the Renaissance in Tuscany.* New York: Architectural Book Publishing Co., [n.d.].

Stern, Giovanni. *Piante Elevazioni Profili e Spaccati Degli Edificj della Villa Suburbana di Guilio III, Pontefice Massimo, Fuori la Porta Flamina.* Rome: Antonia Fulgoni, 1784.

Strack, Heinrich. *Baudenkmaeler rons de XV-XIX jahrhunderts.* Berlin: Verlag von Ernst Wasmuth, 1891.

Stroud, Dorothy. *The Architecture of John Soane.* London: Studio, 1961.

Studio d'Architettura Civile, Sopra gli Ornamenti di Porte e Finestre Tratti da Alcune Fabbriche Insigni di Roma con le Misure Piante Modini e Profili. Rome: Domenico di Rossi, Erede di Gio: Giacomo de Rossi, 1702.

Studio d'Architettura Civile, Sopra Uarj Ornamenti di Cappelle e Diversi Sepolcri, Tratti da Piu Chiese de Roma. Rome: Domenico de Rossi, Erede di Gio: Giocomo di Rossi, 1711.

Studio d'Architettura Civile, Sopra Varie Chiese, Capelle di Roma e Palazzo di Caprarola, et altre Fabbriche con le Loro

Facciate, Spaccati, Piante, e misure. Rome: Domenico de Rossi, Erede di Gio: Giacomo de Rossi, 1721.

Survey of London. London: Greater Country Council (Greater London Council), 1900–1970. 35 vols.

Suys, F.T. *Palais Massini a Rome, Dessine et Publie.* New York: Architectural Book Publishing Co., 1918?

Swan, Abraham. *A Collection of Designs in Architecture, Containing New Plans and Elevations of Houses for General Use.* London: Robert Sayer, 1757. 2 vols.

Swan, Abraham. *The British Architect; or, the Builders Treasury of Staircases.* London: Robert Sayer, 174-?

Tanner, Henry, Jr. *English Interior Woodwork of the XVI, XVII and XVIIIth Centuries.* London: B.T. Batsford, 1902.

Telluccini, Augusto. *Le Decorazioni della gia Reale Palazzina di Caccia di Stupinigi.* Torino: "Itala Aro," 1924.

Thomas, Walter G. *Northern Italian Details.* New York: American Architect, 1917.

Tipping, H. Avray. *English Homes, Period III, Late Tudor and Early Stuart, 1558–1649.* London: Country Life, 1927, 1922. 2 vols.

Tipping, H. Avray. *English Homes, Period V, Early Georgian, 1714–1820.* London: Country Life, 1926.

Tipping, H. Avray. *English Homes, Period IV, Late Stuart, 1649–1714.* London: Country Life, George Newnes; New York: Charles Scribner's Sons, 1920.

Triggs, H. Inigo. *Some Architectural Works of Inigo Jones.* London: B.T. Batsford, 1901.

Triggs, H. Inigo. *The Art of Garden Design in Italy.* New York: Longmans, Green & Co., 1906.

Tuileries Brochures. Chicago: Lodowici-Celadon, 1929–1939. 4 vols.

Turnor, Reginald. *Nineteenth Century Architecture in Britain.* London: B.T. Batsford, 1950.

Valeri, Francesco Malaguizzi. *La Corte di Lodovico il Moro.* Milano: Ulrico Hoepli, 1913, 1915. 2 vols.

Vitruvius Pollio. *Vitruvius: the Ten Books on Architecture.* Translated by Morris Hicky Morgan. *With illustrations and Original Designs Prepared Under the Direction of Herbert Langford Warren.* New York: Dover Publications, 1960.

Ware, Isaac. *A Complete Body of Architecture; Adorned with Plans and Elevations, From Original Designs.* London: Osborn & Shipton, 1756.

Weaver, Lawrence. *Houses and Gardens by E. L. Lutyens.*

London: Country Life, 1914, 1913.

Whiffen, Marcus. *Stuart and Georgian Churches, the Architecture of the Church of England Outside London, 1603–1837*. London: B.T. Batsford, 1947.

Wiener, S. G. *Venetian Houses and Details*. New York: Architectural Book Publishing Co., 1929.

Wittkower, Rudolf. *Architectural Principles in the Age of Humanism*. New York: Random House, 1965, 1962.

Works of Sir John Soane, F.R.S., F.S.A., R.A. (1753–1837). London: The Sir John Soane Museum, [n.d.].

Wren Society. Vols. 1–20. Oxford: The Society, 1924–1943.

Yerbury, F.R. *Georgian Details of Domestic Architecture*. Boston: Houghton Mifflin, 1926.

Zanotto, Francesco. *Le Fabbriche Civile, Ecclesiastiche e Militari di Michele Sanmicheli*. Genova: Mario Morando, 1879.

SCRAPBOOKS

Scrapbook: Italy-Alinari Photographs, 6 vols.

Scrapbook: Italy-Alinari Photographs-Bronze/Iron Work.

Scrapbook: Italy-Alinari Photographs-Ceilings.

Scrapbook: Italy-Alinari Photographs-Churches, 3 vols.

Scrapbook: Italy-Alinari Photographs-Doors.

Scrapbook: Italy-Alinari Photographs-Fountains.

Scrapbook: Italy-Alinari Photographs-Old Office, 12 vols.

Scrapbook: Italy-Alinari Photographs-Paintings; Some Sculpture.

Scrapbook: Italy-Alinari Photographs-Sculpture.

Scrapbook: Italy-Alinari Photographs-Palaces, 2 vols.

Scrapbook: Italy-Alinari Photographs-Renaissance Carved Details; Tombs.

Scrapbook: Italy-Alinari Photographs-Roman Details.

Scrapbook: Italy-Alinari Photographs-Roman Details-Pompeii/Paestum.

Scrapbook: Italy-Alinari Photographs-Villas.

Scrapbook: Italy-Alinari Photographs-Villas/Gardens.

Scrapbook: Italy-Photographs, 3 vols.

Scrapbook: Italy-Photographs-Magazine Clippings.

APPENDIX II

Typical Works not discussed

A complete job list resulted from the research on this book, and only after this list was generated did the scope of Shutze's career emerge. His firms produced over 750 buildings, renovations, and design proposals. The major repository of drawings for these projects is in the Atlanta Historical Society and the Architecture Library at Georgia Tech. Drawings also exist in private collections.

Rather than publishing a complete job list, only certain typical design proposals and buildings have been selected, to indicate the larger number of works that could not be covered within the scope of this book. Other significant works, including major additions to Piedmont Driving Club, are unfortunately not illustrated.

DAVISON/PAXON
(MACY'S DEPARTMENT STORE), 1927
Atlanta, Georgia
Starrett and Van Vleet, New York, Architects
Hentz, Adler and Shutze, Associate Architects

265

WESLEYAN COLLEGE LIBRARY, 1928
Macon, Georgia
Hentz, Adler and Shutze, Architects

266

SINGER BUILDING, 1929
Atlanta, Georgia
Hentz, Adler and Shutze, Architects

267

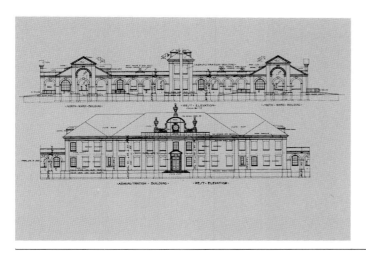

SHRINERS' HOSPITAL FOR CRIPPLED
CHILDREN, 1929
Chicago, Illinois
Hentz, Adler and Shutze, Architects

268

PROPOSED SHOP FRONT FOR J.G. DODSON,
1932
Atlanta, Georgia
Hentz, Adler and Shutze, Architects

269

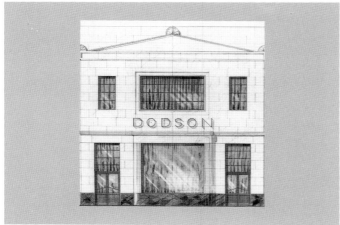

COMMERCE JOURNALISM BUILDING, ca. 1934
University of Georgia
Athens, Georgia
Hentz, Adler and Shutze, Architects

270

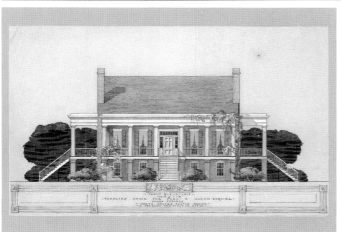

PROPOSED HOUSE FOR THOMAS K. GLENN,
ca. 1940
Sandy Springs, Georgia
Hentz, Adler and Shutze, Architects

271

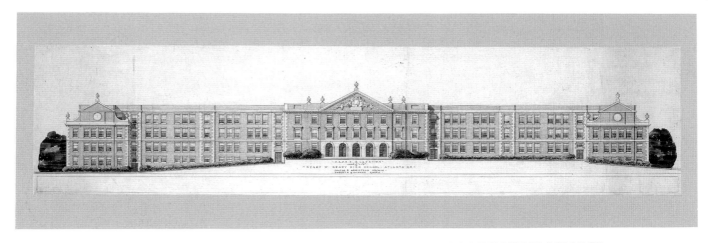

HENRY W. GRADY HIGH SCHOOL, 1923,
1944–49
Atlanta, Georgia
Shutze and Armistead, Architects
Robert and Company

272

EMILY WINSHIP WOODRUFF
MATERNITY CENTER, 1940–1945
Crawford Long Hospital
Atlanta, Georgia
Hentz, Adler and Shutze, Architects
Warren Armistead, Associate

273

RICH MEMORIAL BUILDING, 1946
School of Business Administration
Emory University
Shutze and Armistead, Architects

274

THREE SCHEMES FOR PROPOSED REMODELING OF BUILDING ON MARIETTA STREET FOR CITIZENS AND SOUTHERN NATIONAL BANK, 1950
Atlanta, Georgia
Philip Trammell Shutze, Architect

275

PROPOSED HOUSE FOR EDWARD INMAN, ca. 1960
Andrews Drive
Atlanta, Georgia
Philip Trammell Shutze, Architect

276

PROPOSED SHUTZE BURIAL MONUMENT, 1968
Columbus, Georgia
Philip Trammell Shutze, Architect

277

NOTES

CHAPTER I

1. Joseph B. Mahan, *Columbus: Georgia's Fall Line "Trading Town"* (Northridge, California: Windsor Publications, Inc. 1986): 65–66.
2. Ibid., p. 74. The population of Columbus in 1890 was 17,303; in 1900 it was 17,614.
3. Handwritten memoirs of Daniel C. Schutze dated 1 January 1905, in the family collection of Alvin Cates. The family name was changed to Shutze—dropping the "c"—by the architect's father.
4. Shutze to his mother, Wednesday 31 (of August 1911) p.3, Shutze collection. He made the trip with his classmate Archie Burroughs.
5. Ibid., p.5, Shutze Collection.
6. Hentz had received a degree from Emory University in Atlanta and had worked as a construction superintendent on the high-rise Candler building; after high school, Reid had apprenticed to firms in Macon and Atlanta. Hentz and Reid met in Atlanta and, as the two friends discussed their aspirations to become architects, they concluded that they needed additional academic training. In 1905, they decided to study in Columbia University's architecture program, and after approximately a year, they enrolled in classes at the Ecole des Beaux-Arts in Paris. For financial reasons, Reid studied in Paris for just one year, but Hentz stayed on. In 1909, when Reid returned to Atlanta, the two established a partnership, initially of Norrman, Hentz and Reid, and upon the death of the elder Godfrey L. Norrman, the firm became Hentz and Reid.
   James H. Grady, *Architecture of Neel Reid in Georgia.* (Athens: University of Georgia Press, 1973): x, xi.
7. The history of this important institution may be found in Theodor K. Rohdenburg, *A History of the School of Architecture, Columbia University.* (New York: Columbia University Press, 1954). And in *The Making of an Architect: 1881–1981,* ed. Richard Oliver (New York: Rizzoli, 1981). The passage quoted is by Richard Franz Bach writing in the *Columbia Alumni News* (September, 1912); see Rohdenburg, p. 24.
8. *Annual of the School of Architecture* (Columbia University, 1914).
9. Ibid.

10. These French terms were adopted by American schools of architecture. The *esquisse* is a problem that is given a brief period of 12 to 24 hours in which to finish. The *projet rendu* is a more complex project lasting 6 to 8 weeks.
11. "Young Atlanta Architect Wins Rome Scholarship in Nation-wide Contest," *Atlanta Constitution* (27 June 1915).
12. Ibid.
13. Charles Henry Cheney, "The American Academy in Rome," *Architectural Record,* 31 (1912): 254.
14. Ibid., 244.
15. Ibid., 251.
16. Hough to Aunt Lizzy, 11 April 1916. Hough's papers are held by the family in Conshohocken, Pennsylvania; hereafter, William Hough Collection.
17. The Allyn Cox Collection is held at the Archives of American Art in Washington, D.C.; hereafter, Allyn Cox Collection.
18. Geoffrey Scott's *Architecture of Humanism* (1914) is in print (New York, Norton, 1974) and continues to be studied by architects and historians.
19. Cox to his mother, 30 April 1917, Allyn Cox Collection.
20. Cox to family, 4 March 1917, Allyn Cox Collection.
21. Cox to his father, April 1917, Allyn Cox Collection.
22. American Academy in Rome Regulations no date, p. 5, from AAR in New York City.
23. The Pantheon portico columns are approximately 46 feet 5 inches in height.
24. Hough's sketchbook contains 15 pages of Pantheon drawings; Shutze's sketchbook contains 20 pages. Hough produced a restoration drawing of the Pantheon for his final project. William Hough Collection.
25. Photographs of the Pantheon measuring trip may be found in the Shutze Archive; Smithsonian AAR Archive; and Helena Van Brugh de Kay, "The American Academy in Rome," *The Art World* (1918): 303–07.
26. Geoffrey Scott, op. cit.: 162, 163.
27. Ibid., 26.
28. Shutze credits the American Ambassador, Thomas Nelson Page, with the decision to enlist Academy

fellows in the Red Cross. Shutze collections.

29. Hough to family, 1917. William Hough Collection.
30. The *American National Red Cross Annual Report*, 30 June 1919, p. 109. Records of the Red Cross, National Archives, Washington, D.C.
31. Among the many American architects who volunteered for war service are the well-known architects Guy Lowell, and Chester H. Aldrich of the New York firm of Delano and Aldrich. Major Guy Lowell received a number of military decorations from the Italian government including the Silver Medal of Valor, which was also awarded to Lieutenant Ernest Hemingway. "Personnel of Department of Military Affairs decorated by the Italian Government." Records of the Red Cross.
32. Lucia and Alan Valentine, *The American Academy in Rome, 1894–1969* (Charlottesville: University Press of Virginia): p. 76.
33. Additional discussion of the Howard Theater occurs in Chapter II.
34. Shutze's term had been extended six months due to war service.
35. William Hough Collection.
36. Shutze's personal library contains many volumes on Italian landscape gardening including a small guide to visiting the gardens by Mrs. Aubrey LeBlond. For a list of books on Italian landscape gardening in Shutze's library, see Appendix 1.
37. Cox to his mother, 10 November 1919, Allyn Cox Collection.

CHAPTER II

1. The methods employed by American classical designers have yet to be explored in any great detail. For a comparison with Shutze's methods see: *A Monograph of the Works of McKim, Mead and White 1879–1915 with an essay by Leland Roth* (New York: B. Blom, 1973); William B. O'Neal, *The Work of William Lawrence Bottomley in Richmond* (Charlottesville: University Press of Virginia, 1985); and Richard Pratt, *David Adler* (New York: Lippincott, 1969).
2. The Alinari scrapbooks generally contain 50 pages and are sized 36 by 27 by 5 cm.
3. Most of Neel Reid's books continued as a part of the office library and are now in the Shutze Collection.
4. The Avery Library resulted from an endowment and the donation of the 2,000 volume library of Henry Ogden Avery by his parents, Samuel Putnam Avery and Mary Ogden Avery in 1890. *The Making of an Architect*. Op. cit.: 46, 47.
5. Handwritten notes by Shutze, titled by first line: "In the early forties . . . ,": p. 10 Shutze Collection.
6. The Zanotto folio measures 53 by 36 cm and contains 86 pages of text and 150 pages of plates. The large size of the plates facilitated study. Shutze read and spoke Italian fluently.
7. Academy sketchbook, Shutze Collection. See Chapter I for further details on the measuring trips of the Academy students.

CHAPTER III

1. Shutze made numerous attempts in his later years to develop a chronology of offices and projects from 1920–26. His lists of offices differ in sequence. The chronology used in the text appears to be the one he considered correct. Shutze Collection.
2. The Calhoun Family maintains that Neel Reid designed the house. I find the house uncharacteristic of Reid's other buildings, but stylistically in keeping with Shutze.
3. Known today as the Calhoun-Thornwell house, its original name of Tryggversson was given by Mrs. Calhoun, who was a member of the Trigg family from Chattanooga, Tennessee. The name refers to a Viking ancestor, Olaf Tryggversson, the first King of Norway. Atlantans referred to it as the Pink Palace.
4. Further details of stucco aging were provided by Harry Dwoskin, whose father Morris applied the stucco. Harry Dwoskin told me that the water used in making the stucco was strained through cow manure when I interviewed him 3 August 1987.
   Shutze also wrote cryptic notes on the process. "The powdered colour was mixed with a 'drywall' a clear liquid for use as a water resisting and vehicle - To age - process we applied and when dry—use heavy sacking to weather from dark under projections and cornice—thus grading the colour." Handwritten notes by Shutze to Henry Hope Reed titled "Answering your questions," 16 August 1976, p. 4. Shutze Collection.
5. Ancient classical and Renaissance architects believed certain proportional relationships produced greater beauty than others. These ideal proportions included circle, square, $1:\sqrt{2}$ (square to diagonal of a square), 3:4 (square to square and one third), 2:3 (square to square and one half), 3:5 (square to square and two thirds), 1:2 (double square). Numerous authors recorded this information, the best known being Vitruvius and Palladio. For additional information on the significance of Renaissance proportion see Rudolf Wittkower, *Architectural Principles in the Age of Humanism* (1971). For a detailed analysis of Palladio's use of proportion see Deborah Howard and Malcolm Longar, "Harmonic Proportion and Palladio's Quattro Libri," *Journal of the Society of Architectual Historians* (May 1982): 116–43.
6. Shutze referred to Neel Reid as a delightfully talented amateur. Handwritten notes by Shutze titled "Observations," 1973 November, p. 1, Shutze Collection.
7. For further information on Rich's history see: Henry Givens Baker, *Rich's of Atlanta: The Story of a Store Since 1867* (Atlanta, Georgia: School of Business Administration, Atlanta Division, University of Georgia, 1953).
8. Handwritten notes: "In the early 40's . . . ," p. 22. Shutze toured Europe for the last time from 28 August 1924 when he arrived in Southhampton, England, until a date prior to 28 July 1925, at which time his passport expired, Cates family collection.

9. Handwritten notes by Shutze to Henry Hope Reed titled "Answers to your Questions," no date, p. 2, Shutze Collection.

10. This information is contained in the financial rec ords of Hentz, Reid and Adler and Hentz, Adler and Shutze, Shutze Collection.

11. Robert Tyre Jones (1902–1971) achieved national recognition as a sports figure when he won the grand slam in golf, which is defined as winning in a single year the United States Open, British Open, United States Amateur, and British Amateur Championships. He won these in 1930 and then retired from competetive golf.

12. Like the Calhoun family, the Rhodes family believed Reid was the sole designer of their house. The family acknowledges only Shutze's selection of interior furnishings.

13. Randy Jay, "Design Show House, a Tribute to Architect Philip Trammell Shutze," *Atlanta Journal and Constitution*, 22 April 1979, Rhodes-Robinson File, Atlanta Historical Society.

14. Medora Field Perkerson. "He Made Atlanta beautiful," *The Atlanta Journal Magazine* (20 October 1946), Neel Reid File, Atlanta Historical Society.

15. Handwritten notes by Shutze titled "Observations," November 1973, Shutze Collection.

16. Interview with M. O. Saggus, 1 May 1986.

17. Interview with Virginia Courts, 26 February 1988.

18. James Means (1904–1979) worked for Hertz, Reid and Adler first as an office boy in 1917 and then progressed to draftsman as he received training in the office. He worked with Shutze until 1950 at which time he moved to Albany, Georgia. For additional information see Mrs. John Ray Efird, *The Houses of James Means* (Atlanta: American Cancer Society, 1979).

19. Shutze prepared two handwritten descriptions of the Inman House for use by docents. One is 3 pages, the other is 14 pages and they will hereafter be titled, Inman description, 14 pages and Inman description, 3 pages. "Inman description, 14 pages," pp. 1–3, Shutze Collection.

20. "Inman description, 14 pages," pp. 4–5, Shutze Collection.

21. "Inman description, 3 pages," pp. 2–3, Shutze Collection.

22. "Inman description, 14 pages," p. 12, Shutze Collection.

23. In 1929 Mr. and Mrs. Glenn had commissioned Samuel Inman Cooper to design Glenridge Hall, a 14,000 square foot country estate.

24. Marco Frascari, Associate Professor of Architecture at Georgia Tech, suggested the potential appropriateness of Santa Maria della Salute as a precedent for a Hebrew temple.

25. Rabbi David Marx, *The Temple* (no date). pamphlet. Scagliola is a form of plaster work that imitates stone. In the imitation of marble, pigments are laid in the wet plaster to simulate veining.

26. A complete description of the symbolism of the ornamental plaster details is contained in *The Temple*.

27. The financial records for Hentz, Adler and Shutze indicate the firm devoted 7,152-1/2 hours in 1930 and 4,581-½ hours in 1931 to the C&S project, Shutze Collection.

28. Among his numerous business accomplishments, T. K. Glenn along with Ernest Woodruff and Robert Strickland began the Trust Company of Georgia in the late 1890s; in 1902 he became Vice President of the Georgia Railway and Electric Company (today Georgia Power); in 1921 Chairman of the Board of Atlantic Steel and First National Bank of Atlanta. From Joseph Mayson, *A Brief History of Glenridge Hall: Thomas Kearney Glenn: 1868–1946* (2 pp. typescript, no date).

29. Interview with Lee Patterson Allen, 2 March 1988.

30. The Dismukes house was designed by the Hentz, Reid and Adler firm, but Shutze's initials appear on some sheets.

31. A similar garden theater was included in the landscape design of the Andrew Calhoun house.

32. The following years and project numbers give a representative picture of the effect of the depression on architectual commissions at Hentz, Adler and Shutze. 1929 - 53 projects, 7 prospects; 1931 - 34 projects, 6 prospects; 1932 - 20 projects, 4 prospects; 1933 - 11 projects, 5 prospects; 1934 - 12 projects, 3 prospects; 1935 - 20 projects, 5 prospects; 1936 - 59 projects, 1 prospect; 1937 - 57 projects, 13 prospects. Information from financial records, Shutze Collection.

CHAPTER IV

1. For a discussion of Shutze's response to modernism see Elizabeth Dowling, "A Classicist's Modernism: The Work of Philip Trammell Shutze," *Art Papers*, 11 (Number 4, July/August 1987): 26–30.

2. The first low-income housing project was Techwood Homes of 1936 designed by Barge and Stevens.

   Clark Howell Homes was a joint venture between Hentz, Adler and Shutze with J. Warren Armistead Associate (Principal Architects); A. Ten Eyck Brown, Ivey & Crook, Francis P. Smith (Associate Architects) and Edith Harrison, Grace Campbell (Landscape Architects), Farley Spencer (Associate).

3. Dr. James C. Bryant, Professor at Mercer University, generously shared this information, which will be published in his forthcoming book *The Capital City Club: The First Hundred Years, 1883–1983*.

4. Interview with Athos Menaboni, 21 April 1988. Menaboni was born in Livorno, Italy, in 1895 and studied art before moving to the United States after World War I. His work with Shutze included the Inman house, the Michael house in Macon, the Goodrum house, The Temple, the Mirador Room. For additional information see Athos and Sara Menaboni, *Menaboni's Birds* (New York: Rinehart & Company, 1950).

5. In a letter Shutze described the events leading to his commission to design the Academy of Medicine:

   "In the early forties, war years, the Academy of Medicine with Dr. Howard Haley a very prominent man in his profession and President of the above decided to construct a monument to medicine with a building satisfying its program needs, of sound structure and above all one of dignity and beauty.

Dr. Phinizy Calhoun, a Kind of Dean of physicians, came to see me at the office, obviously disturbed, and stated that the assigned building committee had been working with an architect, with a friend at court, for several months trying to formulate a satisfactory design for the aforesaid. Aside from his doctor interest, he was concerned with housing the fine Calhoun Library.

The architect's preliminary sketches were unsatisfactory and unacceptable—He asked that I design the building for them. I was naturally in a quandary but agreed that, if possible I would help in their dilemma. Dr. Calhoun, Dr. Haley, Mr. Perry whom I knew very pleasantly were all friends—

In such cases it is customary to adopt either one of two methods of solving the problem—No. 1: The existing architect is paid in full, for his services and dismissed. No. 2: is to form an association of the two firms involved with stipulations as to services expected and required of each firm. As requested, we did sketches for the project which met with the approval of the entire committee. The second suggestion was adopted by my firm and Mr. Perry none of whose sketches I ever saw also agreed—

The arrangement in essence, was this. We were the designers—with scaled drawings,plans, elevations, sections, scale details and full sizes and constant supervision—

Mr. Perry was to make all working drawings—engineering and superintenence.

The final result seems entirely successful and has met with general acclaim." Letter from Shutze to Mr. Robertson, handscript, no date, pp. 1, 2. Shutze Collection.

6. Marco Frascari generously shared this information.
7. Letter from Shutze to Mr. Robertson, handscript, no date, p. 3. Shutze collection.
8. The new interior coloration for the Academy of Medicine developed from a study of Soane's residential architecture, particularly Soane's home, 13 Lincoln's Inn Field, London.
9. For Emory University, Shutze designed the Glenn Memorial Church with its Educational Building and Little Chapel, University Gates, Rich Memorial School of Business Administration, Florence Candler Harris Memorial Nurses Hall (1929), Chi Phi and Kappa Alpha Fraternity houses.
10. Information concerning the Whitehead family obtained in interview with Boisfeuillet Jones, 29 July 1987; and with Franklin Garrett in numerous interviews, 1987.

Mrs. Lettie Pate Whitehead Evans' first husband, Joseph B. Whitehead, Sr., invested in Coca-Cola Bottling Companies at the turn of the century. A lawyer and native of Chattanooga, Whitehead and Benjamin Franklin Thomas purchased the bottling rights for Coca-Cola for one dollar from Asa G. Candler, who believed the soft drink's future rested solely on fountain sales.
11. Interview with Mrs. Julian Hightower, 1987 November. Shutze, personally, worked on placing color in the stucco of the Calhoun and Rhodes houses.
12. Craig Bennett, Sr., a Charleston historian, generously pointed out the source of Shutze's inspiration.
13. The Charleston house typically places its narrow facade to the street and has double porches on the garden facade that shade the south face of the house.
14. Interview with M. O. Saggus, 1 May 1986.

CHAPTER V

1. In an interview with Harry Dwoskin, 3 August 1987, he informed me that the businesses were highly regarded for their quality of workmanship and were named Dwoskin, Inc. (wallpaper sales) and Dwoskin Decorating Company (painting and wall furnishing).
2. Harry Dwoskin is another professional who states that Shutze, not Reid, designed the Calhoun house.
3. A similar pavilion appears in the work of the Chicago architect David Adler.
4. Walter McElreath founded the Atlanta Historical Society on 30 June 1926. At his death in 1951, he left his entire estate with the provision that surviving heirs have access to the funds in their lifetimes. The society received access to the funds in 1965. The Swan House was purchased for approximately $500,000 plus the Willis Jones house (interview with Franklin Garrett, 5 August 1987).
5. Shutze knew the gates of the Villa Borghese from his years at the American Academy in Rome. Edward Lawson, Fellow in Landscape Architecture, had produced a measured rendering of the gates, and a copy of this published rendering is in Shutze's Collection.
6. Shutze included this information on the rendering. Shutze Collection.
7. The dimensions of the three rooms in sequence are 30 feet by 30 feet by 30 feet; 30 feet by 60 feet by 30 feet; 30 feet by 30 feet by 30 feet.
8. The Goodrum Greenhouse was destroyed when the property was used for a new house site. The Cates property is now the site of the Ritz Carlton Hotel on Peachtree Road near Lenox Road.
9. "The Decorative Arts," no date. Shutze Collection.
10. Robert Hughes, "Doing Their Own Thing," *Time Magazine*, 8 January 1979: 52.
11. Shutze to Cox, no date, Shutze Collection.
12. Shutze to Spalding, no date, Shutze Collection.
13. William A. Coles, "Introduction," *Classical America IV* (1977): 4.
14. In contrast to Georgia Tech, which never gave Shutze a commission for a building, Emory University commissioned at least seven buildings and the University of Georgia at least three buildings. In part, the tradition of Georgia Tech architecture faculty designing campus buildings (until the practice was declared illegal) may explain this omission.
15 Letter from Cox to Shutze dated 22 March 1982. Shutze Collection. Philip Trammel Shutze died 17 October 1982 at Piedmont Hospital at the age of ninety-two.

INDEX

Illustrations indicated by Italic numbers.

ILLUSTRATION CREDITS